VISUAL QUICKSTART GUIDE

MICROSOFT OFFICE
PowerPoint 2007

FOR WINDOWS

Tom Negrino

Peachpit Press

Visual QuickStart Guide
Microsoft Office PowerPoint 2007 for Windows
Tom Negrino

Peachpit Press

1249 Eighth Street
Berkeley, CA 94710
510/524-2178
510/524-2221 (fax)

Find us on the Web at: www.peachpit.com
Peachpit Press is a division of Pearson Education
To report errors, please send a note to errata@peachpit.com

Copyright © 2008 by Tom Negrino
Editor: Nancy Davis
Production Coordinator: David Van Ness
Compositor: WolfsonDesign
Proofreader: Tracy D. O'Connell
Indexer: FireCrystal Communications
Cover Design: Peachpit Press

ISBN 13: 978-0-321-49840-3
ISBN 10: 0-321-49840-2

9 8 7 6 5 4 3 2 1

Printed and bound in the United States of America

This one goes out to my big sister,
Marie Bevins. Just because.

Special Thanks to:

The folks at Peachpit

Once again, I am indebted to my editor, Nancy Davis, for her fabulous editing skills, and for working on this book even when she really was too busy to do so.

Thanks to David Van Ness for his production expertise.

Everybody else

Thanks to my wife Dori, and my son Sean, for living with me through another book project without strangling me in my sleep.

The soundtrack for this book (hum it along with me!) was graciously provided by my Rhapsody and Pandora subscriptions, and some bouncy pop music that I refuse to identify.

TABLE OF CONTENTS

Index   253

TABLE OF CONTENTS

GETTING STARTED WITH POWERPOINT

Welcome to PowerPoint! PowerPoint 2007, part of the Microsoft Office 2007 package, is an exciting presentation program that can help you create compelling presentations with a minimum of effort. PowerPoint's attractive presentation themes, superior text handling, attractive animations, and excellent graphics capabilities allow you to deliver your ideas with maximum visual impact.

This visual power doesn't come at the price of complexity; it's easy to build a PowerPoint presentation, whether you're a novice speaker or a polished presenter. But don't be fooled into thinking that because PowerPoint is easy to use, it lacks power; there's a lot of substance behind that pretty face.

PowerPoint 2007 runs on Windows (Vista and XP), and has a new file format that allows it to do even more than past versions, but it does a good job of getting along with past versions. PowerPoint 2007 imports from and exports to older PowerPoint formats, so you're able to share your PowerPoint presentations with colleagues who have not yet upgraded, or with your Mac-using colleagues who have Microsoft Office.

In this chapter, you'll learn how to start PowerPoint, see an overview of the program's workspace, customize the PowerPoint interface, and ask the program for help. Let's get started with PowerPoint.

Starting PowerPoint

Starting PowerPoint for the first time is slightly different on Windows Vista or Windows XP. After you open PowerPoint, you can jump right into creating presentations.

To start PowerPoint on Windows Vista:

1. Click the Start menu at the lower-left corner of the screen, then click All Programs.

2. From the list of programs, click the Microsoft Office folder, then click the Microsoft Office PowerPoint 2007 icon (**Figure 1.1**).

   The program launches.

3. The first time you use any of the Office programs, you'll be asked to activate and register the program over the Internet or by telephone.

   You can try out Office before activation. Your Office installation will stop working after 25 uses, unless you activate the program by entering a registration key.

4. Fill out the activation form, then click Activate.

   PowerPoint connects to the Internet and sends your registration information to Microsoft.

   A blank presentation document appears.

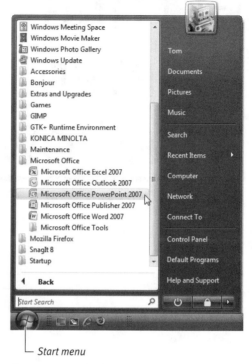

Start menu

Figure 1.1 In Windows Vista, choose PowerPoint from the All Programs list to launch the application.

Figure 1.2 In Windows XP, choose PowerPoint from the cascading All Programs menu.

To start PowerPoint on Windows XP:

1. Click the Start menu at the lower-left corner of the screen, then click All Programs.

2. Navigate through the pop-up menu of program folders to the Microsoft Office folder, then choose Microsoft Office PowerPoint 2007(**Figure 1.2**).

3. The first time you use any of the Office programs, you'll be asked to activate and register the program over the Internet or by telephone.

   You can try out Office before activation. Your Office installation will stop working after 25 uses, unless you activate the program by entering a registration key.

4. Fill out the activation form, then click Activate.

   PowerPoint connects to the Internet and sends your registration information to Microsoft.

   A blank presentation document appears.

✔ Tips

- If you do not activate any of the Office programs after running them 25 times, the programs fall back to Reduced Functionality mode, which allows you to view documents that you have created, but does not allow you to ˻ ˼fy them or create new document˼ ˼ ˼ a registration key unloc˻ restores full functi˻

- When you activ˼ it activates a˺

Exploring the PowerPoint Workspace

The PowerPoint workspace is made up of one main window with several sections (**Figure 1.3**). Let's look at the pieces one by one.

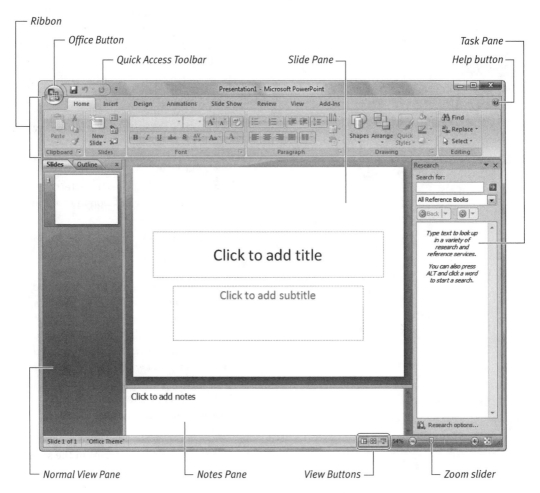

Figure 1.3 The PowerPoint 2007 window.

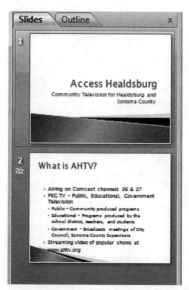

Figure 1.4 The Slides tab of the Normal View Pane shows you thumbnails of your slides.

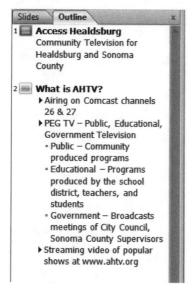

Figure 1.5 The Outline tab of the Normal View Pane shows you the text of your presentation.

If you've used previous versions of PowerPoint, you'll see that things have changed in a big way in Office 2007. The first thing you'll notice is that the menu bar and toolbars are gone. In their place is the *Ribbon*, which contains the tools and commands you'll use to build your presentation.

The idea behind this big change is a good one. Microsoft was forever being asked to add features to the Office programs. But most of the time, those features were already in the programs; they just couldn't be found in the jumble of menus and toolbars (PowerPoint 2003 had 9 menus and 20 toolbars!). So the big makeover (shared by Word 2007, Excel 2007, and Outlook 2007) is designed to make the program's features more *discoverable*; that is, to make them easier to find and use.

The Slide Pane

This is the main PowerPoint document window; it's where you will edit your slides and place graphics, tables, and charts.

The Normal View Pane

The Normal View Pane is the pane at the left edge of the document window. It actually does double duty, showing two different aspects of your presentation. The *Slide tab* shows thumbnails of your slides (**Figure 1.4**).

You can organize slides in this view by dragging slide thumbnails up and down in the presentation.

The second function of the Normal View Pane is the *Outline tab*; in this view the content of your slides appears (**Figure 1.5**). You can create, write, edit, and rearrange your slides and their content in this view. In fact, that's one of the best ways to create a presentation; more on that in Chapter 2.

The Notes Pane

The Notes Pane is where you can enter speaker notes that help you give the presentation; these won't appear on the presentation screen, but they can be viewed on a second display. For example, if you are presenting using a notebook computer and a projector, the notes can appear on the notebook's screen while the presentation runs on the projector.

If you prefer, you can print speaker notes. See Chapter 12 for more information about printing your presentation, including speaker notes.

The Office Button

The Office Button replaces the File menu (**Figure 1.6**). This is where you create, open, close, save, and print documents. It is also how you access PowerPoint's preferences, now renamed PowerPoint Options.

The Ribbon

The Ribbon has eight tabs, each with groups of buttons and pop-up menus with commands and features. More about the Ribbon in the next section.

The Quick Access Toolbar

The customizable Quick Access Toolbar allows you to place frequently used commands just a click away. By default, it contains buttons for Save, Undo, and Redo. Later in this chapter, you'll see how to customize this toolbar.

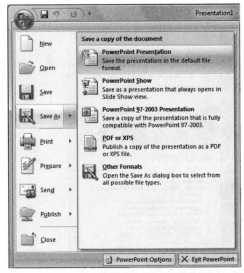

Figure 1.6 The Office Button replaces the familiar File menu, but still pops up a menu with many of the same commands.

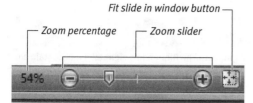

Figure 1.7 Select the magnification of the slide with the Zoom slider.

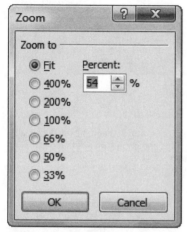

Figure 1.8 If you prefer an old-style dialog to set your Zoom level, click the Zoom percentage next to the Zoom slider.

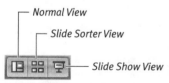

Figure 1.9 The View buttons let you switch between editing and display modes.

The Zoom slider and View buttons

You can zoom into (or out of) the action in the Slide Pane with the Zoom slider at the lower-right corner of the document window (**Figure 1.7**). The Zoom percentage is shown next to the slider; clicking the percentage brings up the Zoom dialog, where you can choose between several standard zoom values (**Figure 1.8**). The Fit choice in the dialog expands or shrinks the slide to fit in the Slide Pane, so you can see all of the slide. There is also a Fit slide in window button next to the Zoom slider that has the same function.

The View Buttons let you switch between three different ways to look at your presentation (**Figure 1.9**). Normal View, as shown in Figure 1.3, has the Normal View Pane on the left, and also displays the Slide Pane and the Notes Pane.

Slide Sorter View allows you to rearrange slides by dragging and dropping them into a different order. Each slide is shown as a thumbnail, along with the slide's number. You'll learn more about this view in Chapter 2.

The Slide Show View starts the slide show, allowing you to preview your presentation full-screen. This is also the view you use to actually give the presentation.

The Task Pane

The Task Pane only appears in specialized circumstances, and changes its contents depending on what you are doing. It probably isn't open on your computer; The Research pane is shown in Figure 1.3 for illustration. Learn more about the Task Pane in Chapter 2.

EXPLORING THE POWERPOINT WORKSPACE

Working with the Ribbon

The Ribbon is the main new part of the Office 2007 interface, so let's go into some detail on how it works. The Ribbon replaces two familiar structures from all previous versions of PowerPoint: menus and toolbars. In their place, there are three new structures:

◆ **Tabs** on the Ribbon are task-oriented. The most common tasks, like adding slides, formatting text, and cutting, copying, and pasting text and graphics, are located on the Home tab. You should be able to figure out which tab to use just by asking yourself "What do I want to do?" and then going to the appropriate tab. So for example, if you wanted to add clip art to a slide, the Insert tab should be your first stop (**Figure 1.10**). There are eight tabs: Home, Insert, Design, Animations, Slide Show, Review, View, and Add-Ins.

◆ **Groups** are areas on each tab that contain related commands. For example, **Figure 1.11** shows the Home tab's Font group.

Commands within a group are usually buttons (as in the Bold and Italic commands in Figure 1.11) or pop-up menus (the Font and Font Size commands). In this book, when I tell you to use a command in PowerPoint, I'll use the name of the tab, followed by the group, then the command. For example, to make some text bold, I'll say, "Select the text, then choose Home > Font > Bold."

Groups automatically expand and contract, depending on the width of the PowerPoint window. If your window size is wide, the whole group appears; narrower windows cause the group to contract, but still show all of its controls, albeit in a more squeezed-together fashion (**Figure 1.12**).

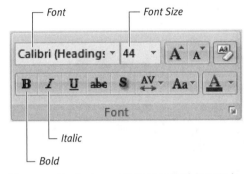

Figure 1.10 The Ribbon has eight tabs that contain all of the tools and commands you'll use to build your presentation in PowerPoint.

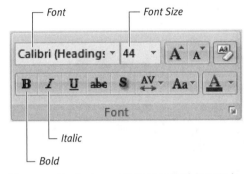

Figure 1.11 The Font group in the Home tab is typical; it contains buttons and pop-up menus that perform related functions.

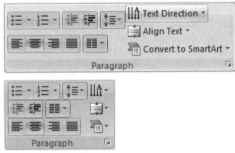

Figure 1.12 Groups automatically grow and shrink to fit in the width of the PowerPoint window. The full width of the Paragraph group shows names for the three pop-up menus (top) while the smaller version collapses the menus to icons (bottom).

Figure 1.13 When needed, contextual tabs appear at the end of the Ribbon, as with these Table Tools tabs.

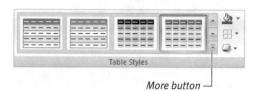

More button —

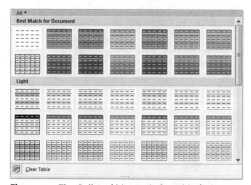

Figure 1.14 The Gallery (this one is for tables) shows you different styles that can be applied to your table with just a click (top). To see more styles (bottom), click the More button.

◆ When you click on some objects to select them, a new tab or tabs may appear on the ribbon. These **contextual tabs** appear to add additional commands to modify the object you have selected, and they go away when you deselect that object. For example, let's say that you've put a table on a slide. When you click on the table, the Table Tools contextual tab appears at the right end of the Ribbon, and it brings along two subtabs: Design and Layout (**Figure 1.13**). The idea is that you only get the tools to work with the table while you are modifying it, and when you no longer need them, the table tools are whisked out of your way.

Some groups contain a **Gallery**, which has many premade styles for whatever you're working with. The gallery in **Figure 1.14** has table styles. You can scroll through a gallery, or you can expand it to see all of the styles it contains by clicking its More button.

Hovering over a thumbnail in the gallery applies a live preview of that design to the selected object (in this case the table). You can easily try out a variety of looks for the object just by moving your mouse, and when you find one that you like, simply click the gallery thumbnail to apply that style to the object.

✔ Tip

■ You can't delete or replace the Ribbon with the menus and toolbars from previous versions of PowerPoint.

WORKING WITH THE RIBBON

Minimizing the Ribbon

The Ribbon is useful because it keeps most of the commands you might want to use right at hand; most commands are no more than two or three clicks away. But the Ribbon's drawback is that it takes up a fair amount of screen real estate, especially on smaller screens like those found on many notebook computers. If you prefer, you can minimize the Ribbon so that it is mostly out of the way, with its tools hidden until you need them. You can temporarily minimize the Ribbon, or you can make the change "permanent."

To minimize the Ribbon:

◆ Double-click the name of the active tab in the Ribbon. The Ribbon disappears, leaving only the tabs (**Figure 1.15**). When you click on a tab, its tools appear, and choosing a command from the tab executes that command, then the tools disappear. To bring the Ribbon back, double-click the name of the active tab again.

To keep the Ribbon minimized:

1. Click the Customize Quick Access Toolbar button at the top of the PowerPoint window (**Figure 1.16**).

   The Customize Quick Access Toolbar menu appears (**Figure 1.17**).

2. Choose Minimize the Ribbon.

   The Ribbon collapses to just the tab names.

✔ Tip

■ Choose Minimize the Ribbon again from the Customize Quick Access Toolbar menu to bring back the full Ribbon.

Figure 1.15 When you minimize the Ribbon, only the tabs remain.

Customize Quick Access Toolbar button ⌐

Figure 1.16 The Quick Access Toolbar can contain whatever commands you need most often.

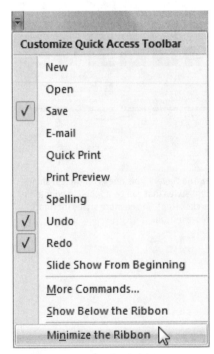

Figure 1.17 The Customize Quick Access Toolbar menu allows you to permanently minimize the Ribbon.

Figure 1.18 The Customize category of the PowerPoint Options dialog lets you customize the Quick Access Toolbar.

Customizing the Quick Access Toolbar

PowerPoint 2007 allows much less user interface customization than previous versions, which let you change any menu or toolbar. But you can customize the Quick Access toolbar, which lets you put the commands you use most often within easy reach.

To customize the Quick Access Toolbar:

1. Click the Customize Quick Access Toolbar button at the top of the PowerPoint window.

   The Customize Quick Access Toolbar menu appears, as in Figure 1.17.

2. The top part of the menu contains common commands that you might want to add to the Quick Access Toolbar. Choose one or more of these to toggle them on or off.

   Icons for the commands you chose appear in the Quick Access Toolbar.

   or

   To get access to a larger set of commands, choose More Commands from the Customize Quick Access Toolbar menu.

   The PowerPoint Options dialog appears, set to the Customize category (**Figure 1.18**). Commands not in the Quick Access Toolbar appear in the list on the left, and commands already in the toolbar appear in the list on the right.

continues on next page

CUSTOMIZING THE QUICK ACCESS TOOLBAR

3. (Optional) To narrow your choices, pick from the Choose commands from pop-up menu (**Figure 1.19**).

The commands in the left-hand list change to reflect your choice.

4. Click to select a command in the left list, then click the Add button in the middle of the dialog.

The command moves to the right-hand list. Repeat this process as needed until you have moved all of the commands you want into the Quick Access Toolbar.

5. Click OK.

The Quick Access Toolbar updates to show your added commands.

Figure 1.19 The Choose commands from pop-up menu lets you narrow your choices of commands to add to the Quick Access Toolbar.

Figure 1.20 Find answers in the PowerPoint Help dialog.

Getting On-Screen Help

PowerPoint also has on-screen Help files. If you have an active Internet connection, the local files are supplemented by additional Help material from Microsoft.

To get help with PowerPoint:

1. Click the Help button (the round button with a ? in it) at the upper-right corner of the PowerPoint window.

   or

   Press F1.

   The PowerPoint Help dialog appears (**Figure 1.20**).

2. Click the topic you want, or enter search text in the search field, then press Enter.

Using Keyboard Shortcuts

If you prefer to use the keyboard, rather than the mouse, to operate PowerPoint (it can often be faster, especially for speedy typists), no problem. You can get to any command in PowerPoint by using a keyboard shortcut, even those found in the Ribbon.

To use keyboard shortcuts:

1. Press and release the Alt key.

KeyTips appear over each feature that is available (**Figure 1.21**).

2. Press the letter shown in the KeyTip for the feature you want.

3. For most choices, you will then see additional KeyTips. For example, if you pressed H for the Home tab in Figure 1.21, KeyTips for the Home tab's features appear (**Figure 1.22**). Press the KeyTips for the command you want.

✔ Tip

■ Of course, there are many "regular" keyboard shortcuts in PowerPoint too. You activate these by holding down the Control key while pressing another key. For example, you can make text bold by pressing Ctrl B. These regular keyboard shortcuts are listed in the PowerPoint Help file, or they appear when you hover the mouse cursor over a command in the Ribbon.

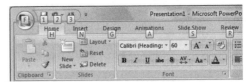

Figure 1.21 KeyTips appear over each feature you can access from the keyboard. Press the corresponding key to activate that feature.

Figure 1.22 When you drill down to the next level, the KeyTips change.

CREATING A
PRESENTATION

A PowerPoint file includes all of the items that make up your presentation, including text, images, and dynamic media, such as movies and sounds. It also includes the set of *slide layouts* for the presentation. Slide layouts are templates for slides that you can use throughout your presentation. Slide layouts contain slide backgrounds and boxes for text and graphics that you'll fill in with your show's content. Slide layouts help you make your presentation look more polished and consistent.

You'll use each different sort of slide layout for a particular purpose in your show. For example, a common slide layout type for the beginning of a presentation is Title Slide, which gives you a large line of type for the presentation's title, centered horizontally and vertically on the slide. Underneath is a smaller line of type for a subtitle, if you want one.

Design elements, such as backgrounds, fonts, and colors, are stored in the presentation's *theme*. A group of slide layouts with one or more themes makes up a *template*, which you can use to build your PowerPoint presentation.

In this chapter, you'll learn how to choose a theme for your presentation; apply a template; add and organize slides; and find the best ways to write a successful presentation.

Choosing a Theme

All PowerPoint presentations have a theme, which defines the overall look and style of the presentation. A theme provides the graphic look for a presentation, and includes a set of backgrounds, fonts, and colors. Think of a theme as a guide from which you can build your presentation.

You can choose a theme when you first create a PowerPoint document, or you can apply one later. You may also change the presentation's theme at any time.

If you choose to begin with a template (see the next section), a theme will already be chosen as part of the template.

To choose a presentation theme:

1. Launch PowerPoint.

   A new window appears, with the default Office Theme, which is a simple theme with a white background (**Figure 2.1**).

2. Click the Design tab in the Ribbon.

   The Design tab tools appear, including the Themes group (**Figure 2.2**).

3. In the Themes group, move your mouse pointer over a theme thumbnail.

   As you hover over a thumbnail, you see a live preview in the Slide Pane of what the theme will look like.

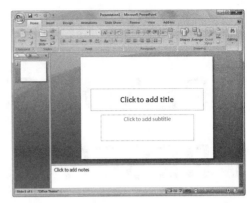

Figure 2.1 The default theme for a new presentation is the Office Theme, with a plain white background.

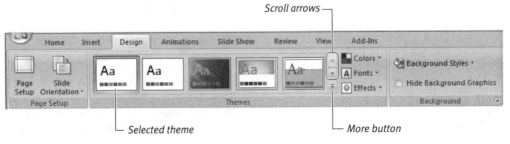

Figure 2.2 You use the Themes group on the Design tab to apply themes.

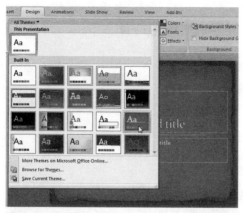

Figure 2.3 The Themes gallery shows the installed themes; as you hover your mouse over a thumbnail, the slide behind it shows a live preview.

Figure 2.4 The PowerPoint window always shows the name of the current theme.

4. If you want to see more themes, scroll in the Themes group, or click the More button. If you use the More button, a gallery appears with the theme choices (**Figure 2.3**).

In the expanded gallery, hovering over thumbnails still shows you the live preview of the theme.

5. Click the thumbnail to apply the theme you want.

PowerPoint applies the theme to your presentation.

✔ Tip

■ The name of the currently selected theme appears in the lower-left corner of the PowerPoint window (**Figure 2.4**).

Starting with a Template

Templates contain not only a theme, but a set of slide layouts. These slide layouts can be customized for a given type of presentation; for example, a presentation that displays mostly photographs would probably include the Picture with Caption slide master, and might omit business-oriented layouts, such as those including tables and charts.

PowerPoint comes with a few templates, and you can access many others on Microsoft Office Online. It's easy to browse, download, and install new templates.

To apply a template:

1. Choose Office Button > New.

   The New Presentation dialog appears, set to the Blank and recent category (**Figure 2.5**).

2. If all you want is a blank presentation, click Create; the dialog will disappear and you'll get a new presentation with the Office Theme applied and the basic set of slide layouts.

   To apply a template, continue with the next steps.

3. Click the Installed Templates category on the left side of the dialog.

   Thumbnails of the installed templates appear in the middle column, with a preview in the right column of the dialog (**Figure 2.6**).

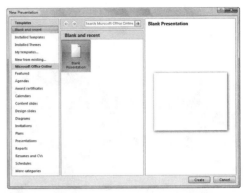

Figure 2.5 By default, PowerPoint creates a blank presentation.

Figure 2.6 You can browse through the installed templates, and get a preview of what they will look like.

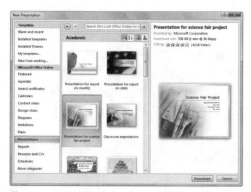

Figure 2.7 Templates from Microsoft Office Online are available in a number of categories, and you can preview what the template will look like.

Figure 2.8 This Science Fair Project template comes with slide backgrounds, font choices, and slide layouts.

4. Scroll to view the installed templates; to apply one of them, click to select it then click Create.

To browse templates on Microsoft Office Online, continue with the next steps.

5. In the left-hand column, click one of the categories under the Microsoft Office Online heading.

Thumbnails of the available templates appear in the middle column, with a preview in the right column of the dialog (**Figure 2.7**).

6. Scroll to view the available templates; to download one of them, click to select it then click Download.

The template downloads and creates a new presentation (**Figure 2.8**).

✔ Tip

■ Downloaded templates will be available in the future in the My templates category of the New Presentation dialog.

Adding Slides

Once you have created a presentation and applied a theme or template, you'll want to add additional slides. You need to first add the slide, then choose the slide layout you want for that slide.

To add slides:

1. Choose Home > Slides > New Slide (**Figure 2.9**).

   The slide appears below the currently selected slide in the Normal View Pane.

2. Choose a slide layout for the new slide from the Layout gallery in the Slides group (**Figure 2.10**).

   Subsequent slides that you create will continue to use the same slide layout, until you change it.

3. Click in a text box placeholder to add text to the slide (**Figure 2.11**), or click one of the icons in the content box to add a table, a chart, graphics, or media clips.

Figure 2.9 Click the New Slide button to add a slide to your presentation.

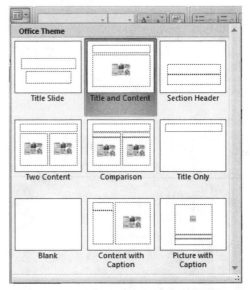

Figure 2.10 These are the slide layouts for the Office Theme; other themes can have different slide layouts.

Figure 2.11 You can add text or other elements in this slide placeholder.

Deleting Slides

Deleting unwanted slides is easy; just select the slide and get rid of it.

To delete slides:

1. In the Normal View Pane, click to select the slide you want to delete.

2. Click the Delete Slide button in the Slides group of the Home tab.

   or

   Press the Backspace or Delete key.

✔ Tip

- If you accidentally delete a slide, immediately click the Undo button in the Quick Access Toolbar, or press Ctrl Z.

Changing Views

The Normal View Pane allows you to view the slides in your presentation in three different views, *Slides View, Outline View,* and *Slide Only View*.

Slides View

This tab in the Normal View Pane shows the slides in your presentation as thumbnails (**Figure 2.12**). The currently selected slide is highlighted with a gold background (you'll have to trust me in this black and white book). Slides View is good for getting an overall view of your presentation, and you can use it to move slides to different spots in your presentation (you'll find more about moving slides later in this chapter).

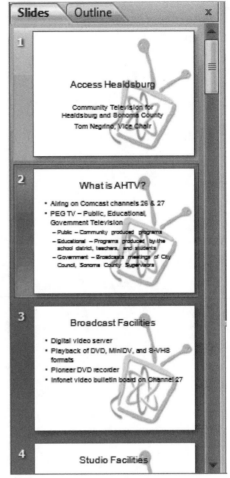

Figure 2.12 The Slides tab in the Normal View Pane shows thumbnails of your slides.

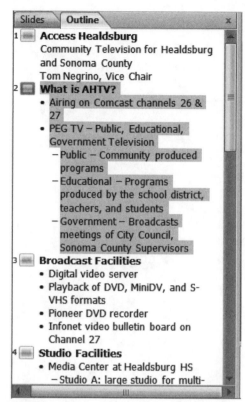

Figure 2.13 The text-only view of your slides in the Outline tab is great for helping you concentrate on the content, rather than the style, of your presentation.

Outline View

The Outline tab in the Normal View Pane displays your presentation as text, with each slide displaying its bullet points as indented text (**Figure 2.13**). Any graphics on your slide do not appear in Outline View. Outline View is useful when you want to concentrate on the words in your presentation, without the distractions of the slide layout or graphics. In fact, I recommend that you create the main structure of your presentations in Outline View. You'll find more about that subject in the "Writing in the Outline" section later in this chapter.

Slide Only View

This view hides the Normal View Pane, displaying only the slide area (and the Notes field). Use this view when you want to concentrate on tweaking the appearance of a slide.

To change views:

◆ Click the Slides or Outline tab at the top of the Normal View Pane.

  or

  To get to the Slide Only View, point at the border between the Normal View Pane and the Slide Pane. When the cursor turns into a double-headed arrow, click and drag the border to the left until the Normal View Pane is eliminated. The easiest way to bring the Normal View Pane back is to click the Normal View button at the bottom of the PowerPoint window.

✔ Tip

■ You can move from one slide to the next in the Slides and Outline Views by using the up arrow and down arrow keys. If you hold down the Shift key while using the arrow keys, you will select multiple slides.

Writing in the Outline

Every good presentation begins with a good outline, and PowerPoint's Outline View is the best and easiest way for you to make better presentations. Using the Outline View helps you keep the presentation logical and structured, because you can easily see the content of slides throughout your presentation. The benefit of working in Outline View is that it lets you create and edit the content of your presentation without focusing on the presentation's appearance, as always seems to happen when you add text directly on the slide. And after all, isn't the content of your presentation its most important aspect?

Another benefit of writing your presentation in the outline is that it is considerably faster than entering text directly on the slides. You can type your text entry in the outline without using the mouse, and any time that you can rely on the keyboard, work tends to get done quicker.

Consider sharing your outline with coworkers, and make changes based on their feedback. When the words are right, that's the time to spice them up with visuals. But first, get the words right.

The flexibility of PowerPoint's Outline View makes it easy to rearrange your ideas as you work on your presentation. PowerPoint provides the tools to move headings up and down, demote headings to subheadings, and promote subheadings to headings

Figure 2.14 In Outline View, slide titles are shown in bold text, and subtitles or bullet points are shown in normal text.

To write your presentation in the outline:

1. If necessary, create a new PowerPoint document.

2. In the Normal View Pane, click the Outline tab.

3. Ignore the slide's entreaty to "Click to add text" and enter your text in the outline.

4. If you're working on a slide layout that has a subtitle or bulleted text, press Return between lines and press Tab to indent the text (**Figure 2.14**).

5. When you're done with a set of bulleted text, press Return, then press Shift-Tab to create a new slide.

   or

   Choose Home > New Slide.

6. Continue creating slides in this fashion until you are done.

✔ Tips

- You can style text in the outline. If you want to make text bold or italic or make other style changes, just select text in the outline and make a choice from the Home tab's Font group.

- When you're working in Outline View, it's a good idea to drag the border between the Normal View Pane and the Slide Pane to the right to make the Outline View as wide as possible. I often make the outline so wide that it crowds out the slide; I don't mind because I want to concentrate on the text, and not be distracted by the styled text and graphics on the slide.

WRITING IN THE OUTLINE

To move headings in the outline:

1. In the Outline View, click on a heading you want to move (**Figure 2.15**).

2. Right-click the mouse.

   The Outlining shortcut menu appears (**Figure 2.16**). This shortcut menu appears only when you're working in the Outline tab of the Normal View Pane.

3. Choose one or more of the commands in this menu:

   ▲ Choose **Promote** to move a heading left, making it a higher outline level, and therefore, more important.

   ▲ Choose **Demote** to move a heading right, reducing its importance.

   ▲ The **Move Up** and **Move Down** choices move a heading and any subheads up or down in the outline.

   ▲ **Collapse** a section to hide (but not delete) all but its main heading; choose **Expand** to show the subheads again. In the submenus, the **Collapse All** and **Expand All** commands collapse and expand all the sections in the entire presentation.

   After a few strategic moves, the outline is better organized (**Figure 2.17**).

What is AHTV?

- PEG TV – Public, Educational, Government Television
- Public – Community produced programs
- Educational – Programs produced by the school district, teachers, and students
- Government – Broadcasts meetings of City Council, Sonoma County Supervisors
- Airing on Comcast channels 26 & 27
- Streaming video of popular shows at www.ahtv.org

Figure 2.15 This text is fine in terms of content, but it could benefit from better organization.

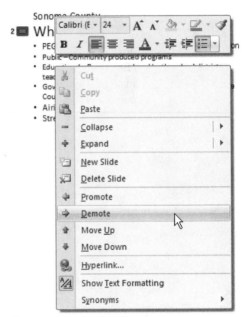

Figure 2.16 Use the Outlining shortcut menu to move headings around.

What is AHTV?

- Airing on Comcast channels 26 & 27
- Streaming video of popular shows at www.ahtv.org
- PEG TV – Public, Educational, Government Television
  - Public – Community produced programs
  - Educational – Programs produced by the school district, teachers, and students
  - Government – Broadcasts meetings of City Council, Sonoma County Supervisors

Figure 2.17 If you compare this to Figure 2.15, you'll see that some headings moved up and other headings became subheads, making the slide clearer.

It's All About the Words

The most important part of your presentation is your message. All of PowerPoint's beautiful themes, slick graphics, and fancy transitions won't save your presentation if you don't have anything compelling to say. The presentation is *you*, not your visual aids. Think of it this way: when you give a presentation, you're telling your audience a story. You know about stories; you've seen and heard thousands of them over the years, from books, movies, television, and real life. So you already know the most important thing about stories: they have to be interesting. If your story isn't, you'll lose your audience. And good stories begin with good, clear writing.

A good story has a conflict between characters or situations. In the course of the story, the conflict is resolved and the story ends. Good presentations hook audiences with a problem, then show the audience how to deal with the problem. When the problem is resolved, the presentation is done.

Outlines are terrific for building stories. I know that you were probably turned off to outlines in some high school English class, but hear me out. Outlines make it easy to see the "bones" of your story. You can see the overall structure of the presentation, and easily see how each slide builds to your conclusion. In an outline, it's a snap to move points around if you see they could be in a better place.

Here's one good way to write (and give) your presentation:

- **Begin at the end.** Odd though it sounds, the first thing you should write is your conclusion. Why? Because it's easier to take a journey when you know where you're going. When you begin with your key message, the audience knows where you're going. This is where you lay out the problem that the rest of your story resolves.

- **Give the background.** You need to give your audience the reasons that your key message is true. So this is where you add the history, research, and other information that lays the groundwork for your story.

- **Make your argument.** Describe how your product or proposed action solves the problem. Share research that bolsters your points. Give examples, and quote sources. Tell stories that show your knowledge of the topic. Convince your audience of the power of your argument. At the end of this portion, give a quick summary, which leads you naturally to...

- **Finish where you started.** Repeat your main point. Then wrap it up and sit down; you've done the job.

One of the most common mistakes people make when writing and giving a presentation is to put the whole presentation on the slides, and then just read the slides aloud. All you're doing is turning the presentation into your speaker's notes, and it tends to put an audience right to sleep. Instead, use your slides to underscore what you're saying. The slides are only one part of the presentation; what *you* have to say should be the focus of the presentation.

Spend the bulk of your time in the writing of your presentation, making sure that the message is strong and that what you're saying tells a compelling story. Then, and only then, you can start working on the look of your presentation.

WRITING IN THE OUTLINE

Writing the Outline in Microsoft Word

PowerPoint's Outline View is adequate in most cases, but when you have a large presentation, it's a good idea to turn to a program that's designed to handle big outlines. Microsoft Word is a good choice. It's got all the power you need to write an outline that you can move to PowerPoint to turn into a great presentation. The program's topics and subtopics correspond to slide titles and bullet points.

The benefit of using Word, however, is that it has many features for organizing ideas that PowerPoint's outliner lacks. For example, Word allows you to sort topics and lets you move topics around with more freedom than PowerPoint allows (**Figure 2.18**).

It's beyond the scope of this chapter to show how to create and work with outlines in Word, but I'll show you how to get information back and forth between the program and PowerPoint.

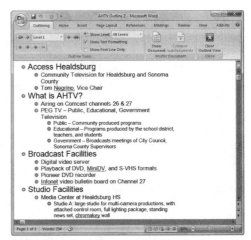

Figure 2.18 Microsoft Word has a great set of outlining tools, and it's easy to move Word outlines to PowerPoint.

Exporting Word outlines to PowerPoint

After you've created an outline in Word's Outline View, all you need to do is save it as a regular Word document; PowerPoint will be able to read it.

To export an outline to PowerPoint:

1. In Word, save the outline you wish to export.

2. Close the document.
   PowerPoint won't let you open the Word document if it is still open in Word.

3. Switch to PowerPoint.

4. Choose Office Button > Open.
   The Open dialog appears.

5. Navigate to the folder where the Word document is, click to select the document, then click Open.
   PowerPoint reads in the Word document and applies the plain, default Office Theme.

Using the Research Tools

When you're writing a presentation, you often need to look up a bit of information here, check a fact there, or use a thesaurus to find a better word. The Research pane, found in all of the Office 2007 applications, gives you instant access to reference materials, both online and on your machine.

To use the Research pane:

1. Click Review > Research.

   The Research pane opens (**Figure 2.19**).

2. Do one of the following:

   ▲ To look up a word, copy it from your outline or slide and paste it into the Search for field in the Research pane, then click the green Start Searching button to look up its definition.

   ▲ Type a word or phrase in the Search for field and press Enter to start a search.

   If you want to use a different reference source (say, you would rather do a thesaurus lookup, or search the online Encarta Encyclopedia), choose the source from the Source pop-up menu (the one directly under the search field) (**Figure 2.20**).

✔ Tips

■ To look up words another way, right-click a word in your presentation, then choose Look Up from the shortcut menu. The word will be transferred to the Research pane and looked up in the reference source you last used.

■ The Research pane has a Translation reference source. You can use it to translate a word or short phrase to and from a wide variety of languages.

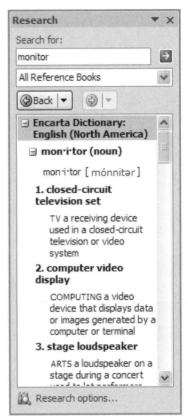

Figure 2.19 Use the Research pane to look up meanings for words or get synonyms.

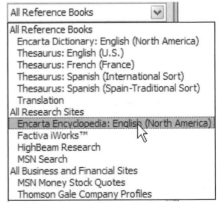

Figure 2.20 You're not limited to just a dictionary and thesaurus—the Research pane has access to many different reference sources.

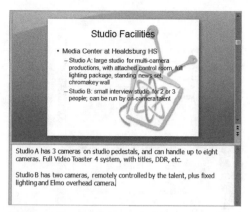

Studio Facilities

• Media Center at Healdsburg HS
  – Studio A: large studio for multi-camera productions, with attached control room, full lighting package, standing news set, chromakey wall
  – Studio B: small interview studio for 2 or 3 people; can be run by on-camera talent

Studio A has 3 cameras on studio pedestals, and can handle up to eight cameras. Full Video Toaster 4 system, with titles, DDR, etc.

Studio B has two cameras, remotely controlled by the talent, plus fixed lighting and Elmo overhead camera.

Figure 2.21 Speaker Notes are just for your benefit; they won't appear while you're giving the presentation.

Adding Speaker Notes

Speaker notes help guide you while you're giving the presentation. You can also print notes along with your slides, for use as audience handouts. PowerPoint's Notes field is completely free form, so you can enter text as you wish. The Notes field is just for text; you can't add graphics or charts to notes.

To add speaker notes:

1. If it isn't already visible, enter Normal View by clicking the Normal View button at the bottom of the PowerPoint window.

2. In the Normal View Pane, select the slide to which you want to add notes.

3. Enter your notes in the Notes field (**Figure 2.21**).

Changing the Slide Order

The Normal View Pane also lets you rearrange the slides in your presentation by dragging the slide's thumbnail up or down in the Normal View Pane.

To rearrange slides:

1. Select the slide that you wish to move.

2. Drag it up or down in the Slide Navigator. A white line with a small rectangle appears, indicating where the slide will go when you release the mouse button (**Figure 2.22**). The cursor also changes to indicate you are moving a slide.

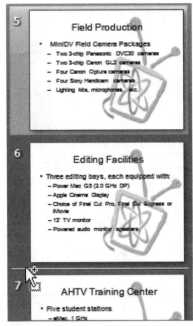

Figure 2.22 The white line above slide number 7 shows where slide 5 will end up when the mouse button is released.

CHANGING THE SLIDE ORDER

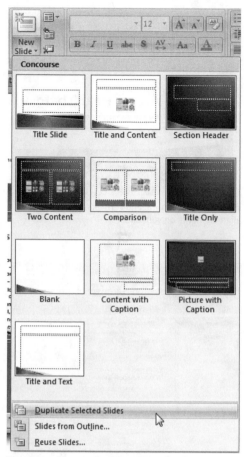

Figure 2.23 You can duplicate slides from the New Slide gallery.

Copying Slides

There are two ways to duplicate slides in PowerPoint. Why might you want to duplicate a slide? The most common reason is that you have added some custom elements to a slide—such as a graphic or a custom text box—that you want to include on a few slides, but that isn't worth saving as a new slide layout.

You can duplicate slides in either the Slides or Outline tabs of the Normal View Pane using the Duplicate command from the Ribbon or using a different Duplicate command in the shortcut menu.

To duplicate slides:

1. In the Normal View Pane, select the slide or slides that you want to copy.

2. Choose Home > Slides > New Slide, then choose Duplicate Selected Slides from the bottom of the gallery (**Figure 2.23**).

   or

   Press Ctrl D.

   or

   Right-click on the slide to bring up the shortcut menu, then choose Duplicate Slide.

   The new slide appears. You can now add text or graphics to the new slide.

✔ Tip

- You can also duplicate slides by cutting or copying and pasting slides in the Normal View Pane.

Using Rulers and Gridlines

When you are placing text and graphics on slides, you'll often want to make sure that objects on slides are aligned to each other or to the boundaries of the slide. Similarly, you might want to make sure that objects are a particular size, especially if you have the objects on more than one slide. This helps you create a consistent-looking presentation. PowerPoint gives you on-screen rulers and gridlines to help you get the job done.

Rulers

The horizontal and vertical rulers can be shown or hidden. You can also set tabs and indents using rulers. See "Setting Text and Bullet Tabs" in Chapter 4 for more information.

To turn on rulers:

1. Choose View > Show/Hide, then select the Ruler checkbox.

   The rulers appear (**Figure 2.24**).

2. To hide the rulers, click in the Ruler checkbox again to clear it.

To hide the vertical ruler:

1. Choose Office Button > PowerPoint Options, then click the Advanced category.

   The PowerPoint Options window appears (**Figure 2.25**).

2. In the Display section, deselect the Show vertical ruler checkbox.

3. Click OK to save your changes.

Figure 2.24 Horizontal and vertical rulers help you align elements on your slide.

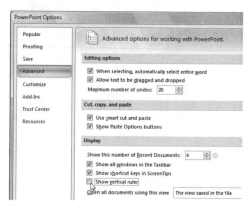

Figure 2.25 If you like, you can turn off the vertical ruler.

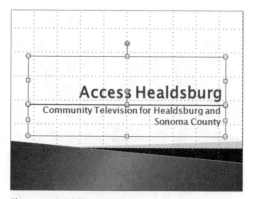

Figure 2.26 Gridlines offer another way to align objects on your slides.

Gridlines

Gridlines help you center and align objects on the slide. When you use gridlines, a grid of small dots appears on the slide, making it easier to align objects. Gridlines do not appear when you are presenting and do not print.

To turn on gridlines:

1. Choose View > Show/Hide, then click to select the Gridlines checkbox.

   The gridlines appear (**Figure 2.26**).

2. To hide the gridlines, choose View > Show/Hide, then clear the checkbox next to Gridlines.

Previewing the Presentation

When you're done writing your presentation, it's often useful to run through it as a slideshow once or twice. This helps you get a feel for the flow of the presentation and almost always shows you places where the presentation could use tightening or better explanation.

After you run the slideshow, you can return to Outline View to tweak the text, or you can begin adding graphics, tables, and charts to your presentation.

To run your presentation:

1. In Normal View, click to select the first slide in the presentation.

2. Click Slide Show > Start Slide Show > From Beginning (**Figure 2.27**).

   or

   Click Slide Show > Start Slide Show > From Current Slide.

   or

   Press F5 .

   The slideshow begins. Click the mouse button or use the right arrow key to advance through your slides.

3. To end the slideshow, press Enter , or − (hyphen).

Figure 2.27 The Start Slide Show group on the Slide Show tab lets you start your show from the beginning or from the current slide.

WORKING WITH SLIDE LAYOUTS

3

A PowerPoint presentation file contains several components that provide its structure and look; we discussed this in Chapter 2, but now we'll go into a bit more depth. The overall structure is provided by the presentation's *template*. Templates are starter documents that can have one or more *slide masters*, which in turn contain all of the *slide layouts*. Slide layouts are blueprints for each of the different kinds of slides in your presentation, such as Title Slide, Title and Content, and the like. Slide layouts define slide attributes such as the position of the title and content placeholders and the slide background.

The look of your presentation is dependent on the *theme*, which specifies colors, fonts, effects, and the bullet styles. You apply the theme to your presentation, and all of the slides in the presentation automatically take on the theme's look, providing a consistent appearance. Themes are shared by other Office 2007 programs including Word, Excel, and Outlook. This helps you maintain a matching look between all of your documents.

When you create a new slide, PowerPoint copies one of the slide layouts, and the objects (text boxes, content placeholders, pictures, tables, or charts) from the slide masters are placed on the new slide. Then all you need to do is put content into the text boxes or graphic boxes. You'll be applying slide layouts much more often than themes or templates. Most of the time you'll use slide layouts without modification, but PowerPoint allows you to customize slide layouts within your presentation to accomodate for your presentation's special needs.

In this chapter, you'll learn about the different slide layout types, as well as how to apply slide layouts to your presentation's slides and change slide layouts.

WORKING WITH SLIDE LAYOUTS

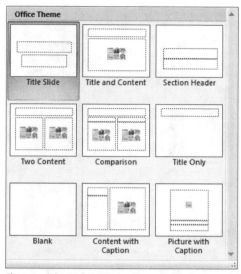

Figure 3.1 The Slide Layout gallery allows you to work with the slide layouts. This example shows all of the layouts in the Office Theme.

Slide Layout Types

PowerPoint templates can contain any number of slide layouts, but in most themes, you'll find at least nine slide layouts, because that's how many slide layouts are included in most of the built-in Office 2007 templates. Templates aren't required to have nine slide layouts; the lower limit is just one slide layout, and I've seen templates from third-party developers that had many more slide layouts from which to choose.

Most of the templates you'll be working with will, however, contain the basic set of nine slide layouts, as shown in **Table 3.1** and **Figure 3.1**. This set contains the slide layouts that you will use most often, so you should become familiar with them and how they are used.

Table 3.1

Slide Layout Types

TYPE	DESCRIPTION
Title Slide	Often the first slide in the presentation. Includes title and subtitle text placeholders.
Title and Content	Includes two placeholders. Top text box uses large type to serve as the slide title; a large content box at the bottom can contain bulleted text, table, chart, SmartArt, picture, clip art, or movie.
Section Header	Similar to Title in that it contains title and subtitle placeholders. Used to set off a section in longer presentations.
Two Content	Has three placeholders: a title and two content boxes.
Comparison	Contains a title, two content boxes, and header text for each content box.
Title Only	Alternate title slide. Includes one text box with large type, justified to the top of the slide.
Blank	Contains only the slide background. Use this for really large or complex graphics.
Content with Caption	Contains one large content box, with a large text box to serve as a title.
Picture with Caption	Contains one large photo placeholder with a large text box to serve as a photo title. Good for photos that need captions.

Applying Slide Layouts

Every slide that you create in your presentation must have an associated slide layout. When you first create a presentation, PowerPoint creates an initial slide based on the first slide layout in the template. The slide is usually a Title slide of some sort.

When you create a second slide in your presentation, PowerPoint automatically switches to the second slide layout in the template. This is usually the Title and Content layout. Subsequently, each new slide you create takes on the slide layout of the slide that was selected when you chose Home > Slides > New Slide in the Ribbon. You can change the slide layout associated with any slide in your presentation. You'll want to do this often; for example, if you add a photo, you'll want to change the slide master to one that contains a photo placeholder.

To apply a slide layout:

1. In the Normal View pane, select the slide for which you want to change the slide layout.

2. From the Home > Slides > Layout gallery, choose the new slide layout (**Figure 3.2**).

   The slide changes to reflect the defaults associated with the new slide layout.

✔ Tip

■ If you have already entered text or graphics on the slide, you might need to adjust them a bit to fit in the new format imposed by the new slide layout.

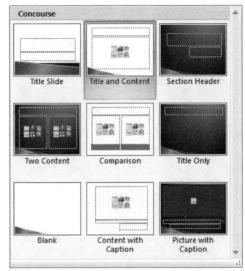

Figure 3.2 The Slide Layout gallery changes depending on the theme you have selected, so you always get a useful preview of what your slide will look like.

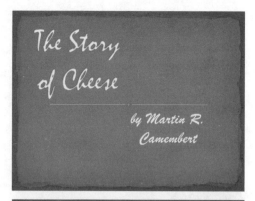

Figure 3.3 A bit of overzealous experimentation led to an overwrought slide (top). Reapplying the master slide resulted in a more dignified presentation (bottom).

Reapplying slide layouts

Sometimes you'll modify a slide, for instance by moving a graphic or text box, and then decide that your changes aren't quite what you want. PowerPoint allows you to reapply the format from the slide layout to your current slide. When you do this, objects on your slide that you moved will return to their positions as defined in the slide layout. If you want to also return the text style or other attributes of the text boxes on the slide to their defaults from the slide layout, you can reset the whole slide.

To reapply a slide layout:

1. In the Normal View pane, select the slide to which you wish to reapply the slide layout styles.

2. Choose the layout again from the Slide Layout gallery.

    The slide and all its objects return to the slide layout's original layout.

To reapply the slide layout and restore text formatting:

1. In the Normal View pane, select the slide to which you wish to reapply the slide layout styles.

2. Choose Home > Slides > Reset.

    The slide and all its objects return to the slide layout's original position and font attributes (**Figure 3.3**).

Modifying Slide Layouts

Most of the time, you'll probably be happy with the theme styles and slide layouts from PowerPoint's built-in selection. But each presentation is different, and sometimes you want to change one or more of the slide masters to better fit the content of your presentation. You'll do this by making changes to one or more of the slide layouts in your presentation in Slide Master View, a special mode that reveals the slide layouts inside the slide master.

The benefit of changing a slide layout in the slide master, rather than on the individual presentation slides, is that layout changes you make in the slide master will appear in all of your presentation's slides that use that slide layout, and this consistency improves the look of your presentation. For instance, you might want to change the size of the content box on the Content with Caption layout to better fit the photographs you want to use. If you changed it on a presentation slide, you would need to repeat those changes on every other Content with Caption slide. But if you change the Content with Caption layout in the slide master, those changes will appear every time you create a new Content with Caption presentation slide, and they'll even be applied to Content with Caption slides you may have created before you modified the slide master.

It's important to understand that modifying a slide layout changes it only for the presentation file you are currently working in; it doesn't modify the copy of the slide layout that is in the template, and your changes also don't modify slide layouts of the same name in other templates.

Figure 3.4 Clicking the Slide Master button opens the Slide Master tab on the Ribbon.

To modify a slide layout:

1. Choose View > Presentation Views > Slide Master (**Figure 3.4**).

   A new tab, the Slide Master tab, appears on the Ribbon, (**Figure 3.5**) and the rest of the PowerPoint screen changes to show the slide master and its associated layouts (**Figure 3.6**).

   continues on next page

Figure 3.5 The Slide Master tab has all of the tools you need to add new slide masters and layouts.

—*Slide layouts*

— *Slide master*　　　　　　　　　　　　　　　　　— *Slide layout being edited*

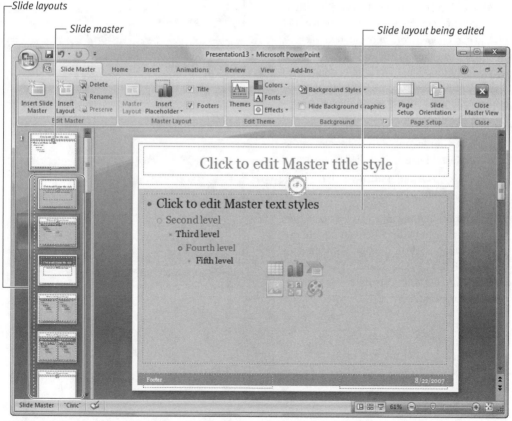

Figure 3.6 When you enter Slide Master view, the whole PowerPoint window changes.

MODIFYING SLIDE LAYOUTS

2. Roll your mouse over the slide layout thumbnails until you find the layout you want to change, then click to select it.

As you roll over each thumbnail, PowerPoint displays a tool tip showing the name of the layout and the number of slides in your presentation that use it.

3. Select elements on the slide layout and modify them.

See Chapter 4 for more information on modifying text boxes, and see Chapter 5 for more information on modifying graphics. If you want to change the slide background, see the next section in this chapter.

or

To add placeholders, choose Slide Master > Master Layout > Insert Placeholder, then choose from the pop-up menu (**Figure 3.7**). You can choose from content, text, picture, chart, table, SmartArt, media, or clip art placeholders. The cursor will change into a crosshair; click on the slide layout and drag the mouse to create a placeholder with the dimensions you want.

4. Format your layout with the tools on the Slide Master tab and its Edit Theme group.

Repeat steps 3 and 4 until you have made all the modifications you want.

5. (Optional) If you want, you can save the modified layout with a new name. Choose Slide Master > Edit Master > Rename (**Figure 3.8**). In the resulting Rename Layout dialog, enter the new layout name, then click Rename.

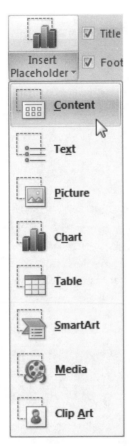

Figure 3.7 This pop-up menu allows you to add different placeholders of the type you select to the slide layout.

Figure 3.8 Click the Rename button to give the slide layout a new name.

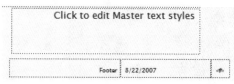

Figure 3.9 All the layouts have footer, date, and slide number placeholders.

6. When you're done making changes to the slide layout, select another slide layout to modify, or choose Slide Master > Close > Close Master View to close the Slide Master tab and continue editing your presentation.

✔ Tip

■ Note that all the slide layouts contain footer, date, and slide number fields (**Figure 3.9**). You can format each of these in the same way you would any other text field.

Number Those Slides!

You use the Header and Footer dialog to enable slide numbering in PowerPoint. In PowerPoint, all the slides are numbered sequentially from the first slide in the presentation to the last.

To set slide numbering, choose Insert > Text > Header and Footer, which opens that dialog (**Figure 3.10**). Click in the text boxes for the items you want to appear, including date and time, the slide number, and the footer. Click "Don't show on title slide" if you want to skip numbering on the first slide. Finally, click Apply (which turns on the selected items on just the current slide) or Apply to All.

You can change the font and style of the slide numbering text box, but you can't control the numbering format. So if you have that urge to use Roman numerals for your slide numbers, you'll have to place them in your slide manually.

Figure 3.10 You can use the Header and Footer dialog to add a date (updated automatically in whatever date format you like, or a fixed date you enter), the slide number, or a footer with any text you want (a copyright notice, for example).

Changing Slide Layout Backgrounds

The most common reason to change a slide layout background is if you have a graphic or photo that doesn't work well with the template's regular background. That's why, in fact, most templates have a Blank slide layout, which you can use as an empty canvas for your content.

Another good reason to change a slide layout's background is so that you can use that changed background for a group of related slides in your presentation. For example, let's say that you're doing a presentation about three different local sports teams, and you'll have several slides per team. For each team, you can use a different background, perhaps keyed to the team's colors. You could change the slide background for each individual slide, but that's more work than necessary. Just create a slide layout with a different background for each team.

To change a slide layout background:

1. Choose View > Presentation Views > Slide Master to display the Slide Master tab in the Ribbon.

   The PowerPoint window changes to Slide Master View.

2. Select the slide layout that you wish to change.

3. (Optional) If, as I recommend, you want to work with a duplicate of the original slide layout, rather than modify the original, right-click and choose Duplicate Layout from the shortcut menu (**Figure 3.11**).

Figure 3.11 To copy the current layout, right-click and choose Duplicate Layout from the shortcut menu.

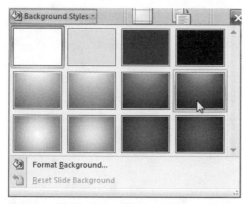

Figure 3.12 The Background Styles gallery provides a selection of gradient backgrounds, but you're not limited to them.

Figure 3.13 The Fill section of the Format Background dialog allows you to add a solid color, a gradient, or a picture or texture as the background.

PowerPoint duplicates the slide layout, allowing you to modify the duplicate. It automatically names the duplicate 1_*layout name*, which probably isn't very useful, so you should right-click on the new duplicate layout and choose Rename Layout from the shortcut menu. Enter a more descriptive name in the Rename Layout dialog, then click Rename.

4. Choose Slide Master > Background > Background Styles, then choose from the style gallery (**Figure 3.12**).

The style gallery includes 12 gradient backgrounds, which may or may not be what you want.

or

Choose Format Background.

The Format Background dialog appears (**Figure 3.13**).

In the Fill category, click Solid fill, Gradient fill, or Picture or texture fill. The dialog options change, depending on your choice.

For example, if you want to use a picture as the background (perhaps one you prepared in a photo editing program), you would choose Picture or texture fill. Then in the Insert from section, click File, choose from the resulting Insert Picture dialog, and then click Open to return to the Format Background dialog and insert the picture you just chose.

5. Click Close to apply and save your changes and return to the slide layout.

continues on next page

CHANGING SLIDE LAYOUT BACKGROUNDS

6. Add any other elements you wish to the background, including placeholders for text, graphics, charts, or tables.

7. When you're done making changes to the slide layout, select another slide layout to modify, or choose Slide Master > Close > Close Master View to close the Slide Master tab and continue editing your presentation.

✔ Tips

■ Once you have placed an element on the background, you can use commands from other tabs to modify it. For example, you can format the font and style of a text box using the Home tab's tools.

■ The Transparency slider in the Format Background dialog is great for fading out photos so they are less obtrusive as backgrounds.

■ You can also create a layered background with, for example, a color or gradient fill in the back, overlaid with an image that doesn't take up the entire slide. See Chapter 5 for more information on using layers with graphics.

GETTING THE TYPE RIGHT

4

In Chapter 2, I strongly suggested that you write most of your presentation in the PowerPoint or Word Outline view. I'm not backing off from that advice; focusing on your presentation's text, rather than the text on your slides, will lead you to write better presentations.

But sooner or later, you will need to work with the text on your slides, and that's what this chapter is all about. For this chapter, at least, I'll assume that you'll be entering text directly onto slides.

PowerPoint showcases Office 2007's improved text handling, layout, and display abilities, and you've got better control over the appearance and style of text within PowerPoint 2007, compared to previous versions. In this chapter, you'll learn how to enter text on slides; style that text as you wish; change the alignment and spacing of text; work with indents and tabs on slides; save time when you're setting text styles; and avoid embarrassing spelling errors.

Adding Title and Body Text

The first slide in your presentation is almost always the title slide, which usually contains two pieces of information: the title of the presentation, and a subtitle, which is where you can put your name and company affiliation (**Figure 4.1**).

In PowerPoint, all text must be in *text boxes*. A text box defines the boundaries of the text. If you have more text than the text box can normally contain (which depends on the size of the text box and the size and style of the text within the box), PowerPoint automatically shrinks the text to fit the box (**Figure 4.2**). When there are multiple lines of text, the text automatically wraps inside text boxes.

Most of the time, you'll use the text boxes provided on the slide layout that you have chosen for your slide, but you can also add your own text boxes to a particular slide, as discussed later in this chapter.

To add title and body text:

1. Open a new presentation file, and apply a design from the Design > Themes group. (See Chapter 2 if you need more information about doing that.)

   PowerPoint creates a new slide based on the first slide layout in the theme file, which is usually the Title Slide layout. The new slide will contain placeholder text for its text boxes, which say, "Click to add title" and "Click to add subtitle" as shown in **Figure 4.3**.

Figure 4.1 The Title slide starts off your presentation.

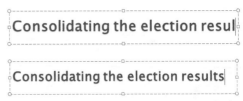

Figure 4.2 When your text won't fit in a text box (top), PowerPoint automatically shrinks the text to fit (bottom).

Figure 4.3 Text boxes in PowerPoint have placeholder text, until you add your own.

2. Click in the title box, which usually contains larger-sized text than the subtitle.

   An insertion point begins blinking in the title box.

3. Type your title.

4. When you're done entering the title, click outside the title box to deselect it, or click in the subtitle box to begin entering your subtitle.

   You'll know you're ready to enter text in the subtitle box when you see the insertion point blinking in that box.

5. Type your subtitle.

6. Click outside the subtitle box to deselect it.

✔ Tips

- It's natural to want to press the Return or Enter when you're done entering text in a PowerPoint text box. But if you do that, PowerPoint inserts another line in the text box.

- If you like, you can place a graphic on your title slide; there's no law saying that it has to include just text. See Chapter 5 for more information about placing graphics on slides.

Entering Bulleted Text

On many slides, you'll use *bulleted text*, which you've seen in most presentations to denote the individual talking points on a slide (**Figure 4.4**). Bulleted text is just that, text preceded by a marker called a bullet. Bullets in PowerPoint can be either text characters, or pictures.

The bulleted text on a slide can have multiple levels, which denote sub-points or sub-topics. For example, you could have text on a slide such as this:

```
Contemporary Folk Music
    Artists
        Kaplansky, Lucy
        Peacock, Alice
        Shindell, Richard
```

Each level of text is subordinate to the level above. On a slide, just as in the text above, that subordination will be shown as indented text. There will be a bullet at each level, preceding the text. In some themes, you'll see different bullets for each indented level (**Figure 4.5**).

When you enter text in a bulleted text box, PowerPoint automatically inserts the bullets whenever you press Enter to begin a new line. Pressing Tab at the beginning of a new line indents that line one level.

On slide layouts with content boxes, PowerPoint allows one bulleted text box per content box. You can manually insert other text boxes, but they can't contain bulleted text (except for text you manually add bullets to with the Home > Paragraph > Bullets button; those bullets don't take on the theme's bullet styles, as shown in **Figure 4.6**).

Figure 4.4 You'll use bulleted text to make your points.

Figure 4.5 Some themes use different colors or shapes of bullets for each bullet level.

Figure 4.6 Free text boxes don't use the same bullets as the presentation's theme.

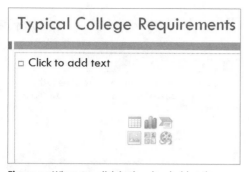

Typical College Requirements

Click to add text

Figure 4.7 When you click in the placeholder, the placeholder text goes away and the insertion point appears.

■ Lynn Miles

✥ Julie Miller

■ Lucinda Williams

Figure 4.8 You can move topics around on your slide with the mouse.

To enter bulleted text:

1. Create a slide with a slide layout containing a content box.

   Typical slide layouts with content boxes include Title and Content, Two Content, Comparison, and Content with Caption.

2. In the text box with the "Click to add text" placeholder, click to place the insertion point (**Figure 4.7**).

3. Enter your text.

   If your entry is too long, it will wrap within the text box, with the default left text alignment.

4. Press Return to begin a new line.

   PowerPoint automatically inserts a new bullet at the beginning of the line.

5. (Optional) To indent text one level, press Tab before you begin typing on a new line.

✔ Tips

■ Press [Shift][Tab] with the insertion point placed at the start of a line of text to remove one level of indenting.

■ You can move text around with the mouse by pointing at a bullet, which turns the mouse cursor into a four-headed arrow (**Figure 4.8**). Click and drag the bullet point, which moves the bullet and its associated text together, to rearrange the text on the slide.

ENTERING BULLETED TEXT

Entering Special Characters

It's common to need to add special characters to your slides, such as the copyright, trademark or currency symbols. These characters aren't on your keyboard, so PowerPoint gives you another way to add them.

To enter special characters:

1. Click in a text box to set the insertion point.

2. Choose Insert > Text > Symbol (**Figure 4.9**).

    The Symbol dialog appears (**Figure 4.10**).

3. Recently used symbols are listed at the bottom of the dialog; click the one you want to select it.

    or

    Scroll through the list of symbols at the top of the dialog to find the one you want, then click to select it.

4. Click Insert.

    Nothing appears to happen, but PowerPoint has inserted the character at the insertion point.

5. Click the window's Close box.

    The character you inserted appears on the slide (**Figure 4.11**).

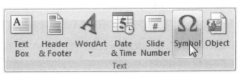

Figure 4.9 Clicking the Symbol button opens the Symbol dialog box, which you use to insert special characters.

Figure 4.10 Click the symbol you want, then click Insert.

© 2008, WonderWidget Corp.

Figure 4.11 The copyright symbol was inserted using the Symbol dialog.

New Napier Arch, Napier, New Zealand

Figure 4.12 This free text box works fine as a picture caption.

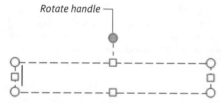
Rotate handle

Figure 4.13 When you see the insertion point, you can type your text into the text box.

Adding Text Boxes

Besides the bulleted text boxes found on many slide layouts, you can also add your own text boxes to slides. These "free" text boxes can be used wherever you need extra text on a slide. For example, you can use a text box as a picture caption (**Figure 4.12**).

You format the text in a text box in much the same way that you format any text (for more about this, see "Formatting Text," later in this chapter), but there is a special dialog box that you can use, too.

To add a text box:

1. On the slide where you want to add the text box, choose Insert > Text > Text Box. The cursor changes into a crosshair.

2. Click and drag the cursor, drawing the text box to the size you want and putting it where you want to position it on the slide.

3. Release the mouse button to create the text box, which displays an insertion point, then enter your text (**Figure 4.13**).

✔ Tips

■ Free text boxes automatically grow or shrink vertically to handle the length of your text. You can resize them using their selection handles, just like most other objects in PowerPoint.

■ If you want to rotate the text box, click and drag the green Rotate handle above the box. The cursor turns into a curved arrow, and you can rotate the box freely.

ADDING TEXT BOXES

To format text in a text box:

1. Right-click the text box, then choose Format Shape from the resulting short-cut menu.

   The Format Shape dialog appears.

2. Click the Text Box category (**Figure 4.14**).

3. Make adjustments to your text.

   You can change the vertical alignment, the text direction (horizontal or rotated in 90 degree increments), the way the text is automatically fit in the box, the margins of the text within the box, or the number of columns in the text box.

4. When you are done formatting, click Close.

Figure 4.14 You can tweak properties of your text box with the Text Box category of the Format Shape dialog.

Figure 4.15 The text in this screenshot comes from two free text boxes overlaid on a picture.

Layering Text

Once text has been created in text boxes on a slide, the text box can be treated, in many ways, as if it were a graphic object. You can move text boxes around and rotate them, apply drop shadows and graphic fills, and change the opacity of the text. For more about those topics, see Chapter 5, and remember that the same tools can be applied equally to graphics and text boxes.

There's another useful text manipulation you can do, and that is to layer text boxes with the other elements on the slide. Imagine that each element—text, graphics, movies, shapes, etc.—on the slide is in its own layer on the slide, with the slide layout making up the layer that's in the back. You can move each element forward or back in the stack. It's possible to get some interesting results by layering, as shown in **Figure 4.15**.

To layer text boxes:

1. Create the text boxes on the slide that you want to layer.

   These boxes can include the Title and Content boxes.

2. Select a text box.

   The Drawing Tools contextual tab appears in the Ribbon.

3. To move the text box backward in the layer order, choose Drawing Tools > Format > Arrange > Send to Back (or click the arrow next to the button and choose Send Backwards from the pop-up menu).

   or

   To move the text box forward in the layer order, choose Drawing Tools > Format > Arrange > Bring to Front (or click the arrow next to the button and choose Bring Forward from the pop-up menu).

   The selected item moves as you command.

Formatting Text

PowerPoint does a good job of showing off the improved font rendering capabilities in Office 2007 and Windows Vista. You can scale text with no loss of quality, so your presentations will remain readable (unless you make the text too small for people in the back row!).

The main tools you'll use to work with fonts are in the Font and Paragraph groups on the Home tab of the Ribbon (**Figures 4.16** and **4.17**). These tools are similar to the ones in the other Office 2007 applications. Because great-looking text is so vital to a good presentation, I'll be discussing the text tools in depth.

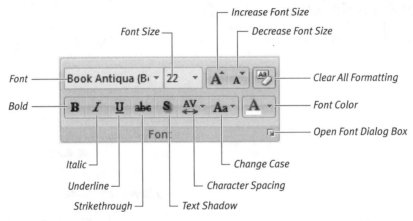

Figure 4.16 Most of your font stylings are done using the Font group on the Home tab of the Ribbon.

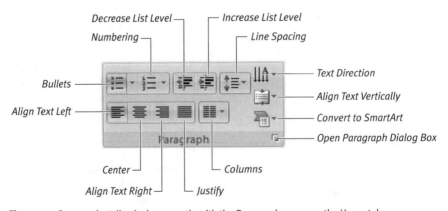

Figure 4.17 Paragraph styling is done mostly with the Paragraph group on the Home tab.

Figure 4.18 Choose the typeface you want from the Font menu.

To change fonts in a text box:

1. Select the text you want to change.

2. Choose Home > Font > Font, then choose the font you want from the pop-up menu (**Figure 4.18**).

   As you hover over a font, the text shows you a live preview of the change. Click a font to select it, and the selected text changes.

   Notice how PowerPoint lists the fonts used in the theme design at the top, other fonts that have been recently used next, then all the fonts in your system last. All the fonts are shown as previews, rather than just a plain menu font.

✔ Tip

■ In the Font menu, you can also see what format a font is by looking at the icon next to the font name. The double-T icon stands for TrueType, and the stylized O stands for OpenType. A discussion of these two font formats is beyond the scope of this book; I recommend that you read the Wikipedia entries for both formats.

Changing font sizes

Like changing fonts, changing font sizes is just a matter of selecting text boxes or text and making your choice from the Font window.

To change the size of type:

1. Select the text you want to change.

2. Choose Home > Font > Font Size, then choose the size you want from the pop-up menu.

    As you hover over a font size, the text shows you a live preview of the size change. Click a size to select it, and the selected text changes.

    or

    Choose Home > Font > Increase Font Size, or press Ctrl Shift >.

    or

    Choose Home > Font > Decrease Font Size, or press Ctrl Shift <.

    These two buttons change the font size up or down in the same increments that they are listed in the Font Size menu. So for instance, clicking Increase Font Size on 24-point text jumps the text size to 28 points, and clicking Decrease Font Size on that same 24-point text shrinks the text to 20 points.

Figure 4.19 You can use the Font dialog to make several font style changes at the same time.

Setting font styles

There are several font styles that you can set using the Font group, including bold, italic, underline, strikethrough, and shadow. There are also additional styles accessible from the Font dialog.

To set basic font styles:

1. In a text box, select the text that you want to style.

2. Click on the style button you want from the choices in Home > Font.

   or

   To make text bold face, press Ctrl B.

   or

   To make text italic, press Ctrl I.

   or

   To underline the text, press Ctrl U.

   The text changes as you command.

To set additional font styles:

1. Select the text that you want to style.

2. At the lower-right corner of the Font group, click the Open Font Dialog Box button.

   The Font dialog appears (**Figure 4.19**). The additional font styles available in this dialog include your choice of underline style and color; double strikethrough; superscript; subscript; small caps; all caps; and the ability to equalize the character height.

3. Make your choices in the Font dialog, then click OK to apply your changes.

✔ Tip

■ You can also set superscripts and subscripts from the keyboard; for superscript, press Ctrl Shift + (plus sign), and for subscript, press Ctrl Shift = (equal sign)

FORMATTING TEXT

Using Equations in PowerPoint

PowerPoint is fine for creating basic superscripts and subscripts, but its shortcomings in creating complex equations will make mathematicians, scientists, and engineers throw up their hands in horror. PowerPoint's built-in text tools just aren't made for specialized formatting of that complexity.

The solution is to use other applications to create an equation, save it as an object, then place the equation into your presentation. Microsoft provides a good basic program for equation creation, Microsoft Equation Editor, which is part of the default installation of Office. The Equation Editor does a decent job for light-duty equation wranglers. To use it, choose Insert > Object, then choose Microsoft Equation from the resulting dialog. The Equation Editor will open, and you can type your equation into it, using the editor's tools to give it that equation-y goodness (**Figure 4.20**). Then choose File > Exit and return to [presentation name]. You'll need to resize the graphic, but the result looks good (**Figure 4.21**).

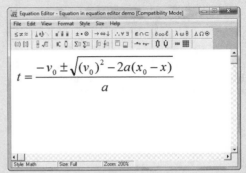

Figure 4.20 The Microsoft Equation Editor is a handy way to get equations into PowerPoint.

If you have hard-core equation needs, consider upgrading to MathType ($97; www.dessci.com), which is made by Design Science, the same company that provides Equation Editor for Microsoft. MathType contains many more symbols, templates, and specialized math fonts than Equation Editor. You may also want to consider turning to the LaTeX equation typesetting system. There are free, open source software implementations of LaTeX for Windows; perhaps the best known is MiKTeX, which you can find at www.miktex.org.

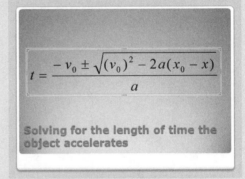

Figure 4.21 This equation was created in the Microsoft Equation Editor, then placed into PowerPoint. After scaling the graphic up to a size where it will look good on a slide, the result is quite acceptable.

Figure 4.22 The five choices for text capitalization.

Changing text case

Sometimes you accidentally press your Caps Lock key, and type an entry in all uppercase. Or perhaps you purposely made a title uppercase for effect, then later decide you don't like that effect. Rather than retyping the offending entry, use PowerPoint's Change Case feature to apply the capitalization you want.

To change text case:

1. Select the text that needs its case changed.

2. Choose Home > Font > Change Case, then choose the capitalization you want from the pop-up menu (**Figure 4.22**).

   Your choices are:
   - ▲ Sentence case.
   - ▲ lowercase
   - ▲ UPPERCASE
   - ▲ Capitalize Each Word
   - ▲ tOGGLE cASE

   The text changes.

FORMATTING TEXT

Modifying Text Color

There are different color pickers you can use to apply colors to text.

To change the color of text:

1. Select the text whose color you wish to change.

2. Click the Font Color button in the Font group.

   The Colors pop-up menu appears (**Figure 4.23**).

3. Pick one of the Theme Colors or the Standard Colors to select the color you want.

   The text changes color.

4. (Optional) If you want to use a color picker to choose a color not in the pop-up menu, choose More Colors.

   The Colors dialog appears, set to the Standard tab (**Figure 4.24**). You also have the choice of a different color picker on the Custom tab.

5. (Optional) Choose a color from one of the color pickers, then click OK.

   The text changes color.

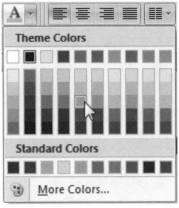

Figure 4.23 Use the Colors pop-up menu to choose from one of the compatible theme colors, standard colors, or choose More Colors to open the color picker.

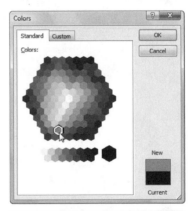

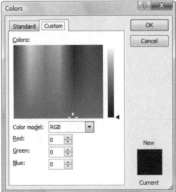

Figure 4.24 The Standard (top) and Custom (bottom) color pickers allow you to pick colors not listed in the Colors pop-up menu.

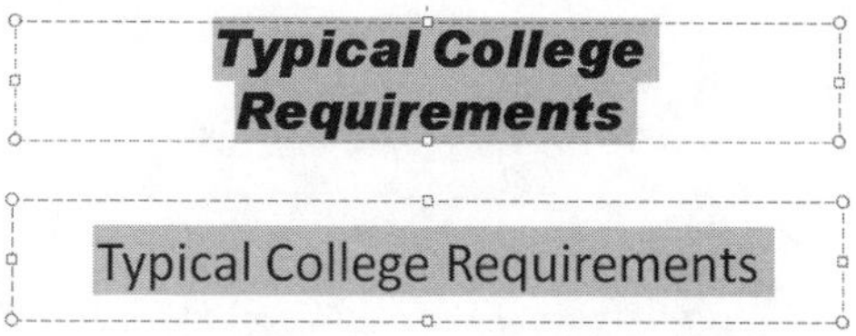

Figure 4.25 If you have over-styled your text (top), you can easily clear the formatting and return it to the default theme style (bottom).

Removing Font Formatting

If you make a bunch of font style changes, then decide that you really prefer the default font styling of the theme, you don't have to go back and re-style the text. Instead, you can simply remove the font formatting.

To remove font formatting:

1. Select the text that you want to return to the default font style for your presentation's theme.

2. Choose Home > Font > Clear All Formatting.

   The text returns to the theme's default style (**Figure 4.25**).

Changing Text Alignment

PowerPoint has two ways to control text alignment. You can set horizontal alignment in the four standard ways: Left, Center, Right, and Justified (**Figure 4.26**). You can also set vertical alignment, which controls where the text is placed (Top, Middle, Bottom) within its text box (**Figure 4.27**). You'll use the Paragraph group in the Home tab to do the job.

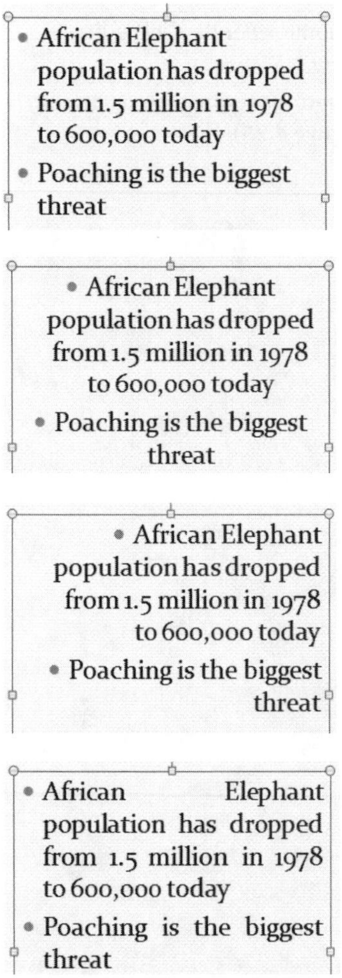

- African Elephant population has dropped from 1.5 million in 1978 to 600,000 today
- Poaching is the biggest threat

- 29 total lifts
  - 10 Quads
  - 7 Triple chairs
  - 7 Double chairs
  - 5 Surface lifts

- African Elephant population has dropped from 1.5 million in 1978 to 600,000 today
- Poaching is the biggest threat

- 29 total lifts
  - 10 Quads
  - 7 Triple chairs
  - 7 Double chairs
  - 5 Surface lifts

- African Elephant population has dropped from 1.5 million in 1978 to 600,000 today
- Poaching is the biggest threat

- African Elephant population has dropped from 1.5 million in 1978 to 600,000 today
- Poaching is the biggest threat

- 29 total lifts
  - 10 Quads
  - 7 Triple chairs
  - 7 Double chairs
  - 5 Surface lifts

Figure 4.26 Horizontal text alignment within a text box, showing (from top to bottom) Left, Center, Right, and Justified text alignments.

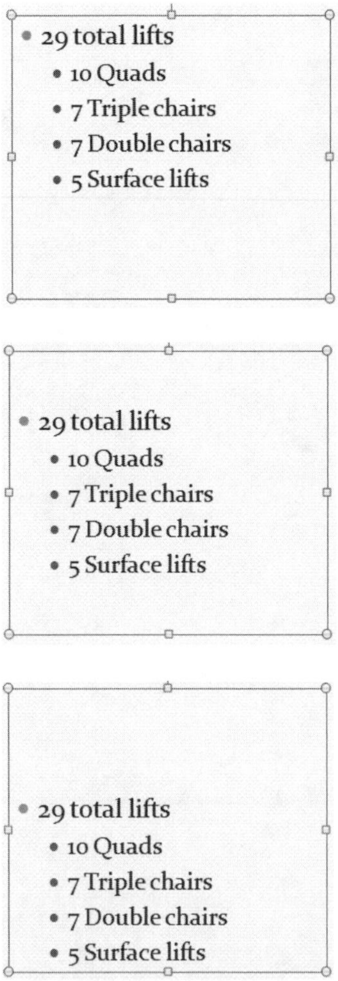

Figure 4.27 Vertical text alignment within a text box. From top to bottom: Top, Middle, and Bottom alignments.

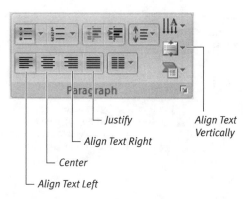

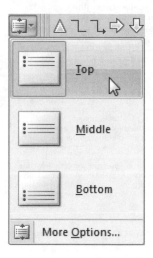

Justify

Align Text Right

Center

Align Text Left

Align Text Vertically

Figure 4.28 Use the buttons in the Paragraph group to set horizontal and vertical alignment.

Top

Middle

Bottom

More Options...

Figure 4.29 Use this pop-up menu to set vertical spacing within a text box.

To set horizontal text alignment:

1. On your slide, select the text whose alignment you wish to change.

2. Click the appropriate horizontal alignment button in the Home > Paragraph group (**Figure 4.28**).

   The text alignment changes.

✔ Tip

■ You can also set horizontal text alignment from the keyboard with the following keyboard shortcuts:

   Left align: Ctrl L

   Center: Ctrl E

   Right align: Ctrl R

   Justify: Ctrl J

To set vertical text alignment:

1. On your slide, select the text whose alignment you wish to change.

2. Choose the alignment you want from the pop-up menu at Home > Paragraph > Align Text Vertically (**Figure 4.29**).

   The text alignment changes.

CHANGING TEXT ALIGNMENT

Creating Text Columns

Within a text box, PowerPoint allows you to create columns of text. You can create two, three, or even more columns in a text box, though for slides, more than two columns will rarely look good.

To arrange your text in columns:

1. Click on a text box to select it.

2. Choose Home > Paragraph > Columns, then choose the number of columns you want from the pop-up menu (**Figure 4.30**).

   The text changes (**Figure 4.31**).

3. (Optional) to add more than three columns, choose More Columns from the pop-up menu. The Columns dialog appears (**Figure 4.32**). Set the number of columns and the spacing between them, then click OK.

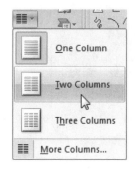

Figure 4.30
This pop-up menu allows you to arrange your text in columns within a text box.

- A favorite trick of spammers (and some legitimate businesses) is *web bugs*, which are images embedded into email and Web pages. Merely loading the image by viewing it triggers the web bug, which may report back to the spammer if and when a particular email message has been read and possibly your IP address.
- To protect you from web bugs (not to mention offensive graphics like pornography in spam), Entourage doesn't downloads pictures in email messages by default; instead, you can click a link in the header of the email to display pictures, if you think the email is innocuous.

- A favorite trick of spammers (and some legitimate businesses) is *web bugs*, which are images embedded into email and Web pages. Merely loading the image by viewing it triggers the web bug, which may report back to the spammer if and when a particular email message has been read and possibly your IP address.
- To protect you from web bugs (not to mention offensive graphics like pornography in spam), Entourage doesn't downloads pictures in email messages by default; instead, you can click a link in the header of the email to display pictures, if you think the email is innocuous.

Figure 4.31 This text has been set into columns.

Columns

Number: 4

Spacing: 0"

OK   Cancel

Figure 4.32 If you need more control over the number or spacing of columns, use the Columns dialog.

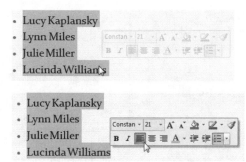

Figure 4.33 The Mini toolbar begins to appear after you select text (top) and fully comes into view when you move the cursor over it (bottom).

Using the Mini Toolbar

When you select text in PowerPoint, a small semitransparent toolbar appears near your cursor. This is the Mini toolbar, and if you move your cursor over the Mini toolbar, it will come completely into view (**Figure 4.33**). The Mini toolbar makes it easy to style text without having to resort to the Ribbon. You can use it to set fonts, font size, text color, bold, italic, text alignment, create bulleted lists, and increase or decrease bullet indent.

To use the Mini toolbar:

1. Select any text.

   The Mini toolbar appears, but remains dim.

2. Move the cursor over the Mini toolbar.

   The Mini toolbar comes completely into view.

3. Use one or more of the tools in the Mini toolbar to style your text.

Adjusting Text Spacing

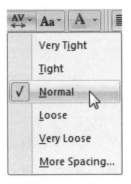

You have control over two attributes of the spacing of your text. *Character spacing* affects the amount of space that PowerPoint puts between the characters within a line. *Line spacing* is the amount of space between two or more lines of text.

Two other adjustments, *before and after paragraph spacing*, control the spacing between paragraphs on the slide.

Figure 4.34 Use this pop-up menu to control character spacing.

To change character spacing:

1. Select the text that you wish to change.

2. Choose Home > Font > Character Spacing, then pick from the pop-up menu (**Figure 4.34**). Your choices range from Very Tight to Very Loose.

   The text changes (**Figure 4.35**).

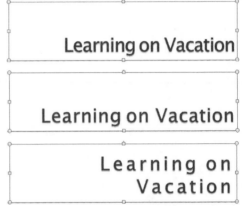

Figure 4.35 The effects of increasing character spacing, from Very Tight (top), Normal (middle), to Very Loose (bottom). At the Very Loose setting, the text won't fit in the text box anymore, and is forced to wrap.

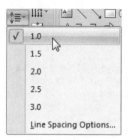

Figure 4.36 Use this pop-up menu to control line spacing.

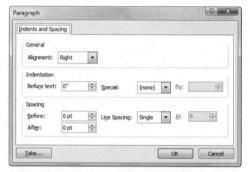

Figure 4.37 You can use the Spacing section of this dialog to increase or decrease the space above or below a paragraph.

To change line spacing:

1. Select the text that you wish to change.

2. Choose Home > Paragraph > Line Spacing, then pick from the pop-up menu (**Figure 4.36**).

   The text changes.

To change paragraph spacing:

1. Select the text that you wish to change.

2. At the lower-right corner of the Home > Paragraph group, click the Open Paragraph Dialog Box button.

   The Paragraph dialog appears (**Figure 4.37**).

3. In the Spacing section of the dialog, change the values in the Before or After fields.

   The text changes.

✔ Tips

■ Be aware of the differences when using line spacing and paragraph spacing. You'll use line spacing most often when you want to change line spacing within a free text box. Paragraph spacing is more often used when you want to compress the amount of vertical space one or more paragraphs takes up on the slide.

■ Remember that PowerPoint treats each bullet point on a slide as its own paragraph.

Copying and Pasting Font Formatting

Another handy timesaving feature is PowerPoint's ability to copy and paste font styles, which includes most formatting that you have applied to text, including the font, font size, color, and character spacing (though not line spacing). The Format Painter allows you to "pick up" formatting from some text and "paint" it onto the destination text.

Figure 4.38 The Format Painter is one of PowerPoint's most useful tools.

Figure 4.39 You can paint formats that you've picked up with the Format Painter on to other text when the cursor changes into this icon.

To copy and paste font styles:

1. Select the text that has the formatting you want to copy.

2. Click Home > Clipboard > Format Painter (**Figure 4.38**).

   The mouse cursor turns into an I-beam with a paintbrush (**Figure 4.39**).

3. Select the destination text.

   The text takes on the format of the text that you selected in Step 1.

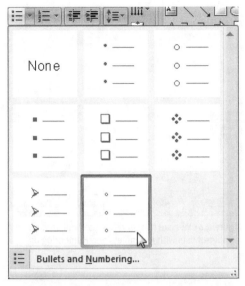

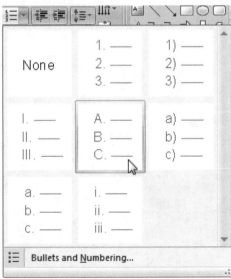

Figure 4.40 The Bullets (top) and Numbering (bottom) galleries.

Setting Bullet and Number Styles

The bullets that appear at the beginning of lines of bulleted text can be customized. You can mix different bullet styles within a group of bullets, and bullets can be either text characters or pictures.

Most of the time, you'll probably use the bullet styles that are part of the theme for the presentation, because those styles have been designed to match the look of the theme. But it's sometimes useful to customize bullets for particular slides. For example, on a slide that discusses financial matters, you could change the usual image bullets into dollar signs to emphasize your point.

To set bullet and number styles:

1. To apply a bullet or number style to an entire bulleted text box, click once in the box to select it.

   or

   To apply a bullet or number style to multiple lines inside a bulleted text box, select the lines.

   or

   To apply a bullet or number style to a single line, click twice to set the insertion point in the line.

2. From Home > Paragraph > Bullets or Home > Paragraph > Numbering, choose the type of bullet or number style you want from the pop-up menu (**Figure 4.40**). The selection changes.

continues on next page

SETTING BULLET AND NUMBER STYLES

3. (Optional) For additional customization, choose Bullets and Numbering from either of the Bullet or Numbering pop-up menus.

The Bullets and Numbering dialog appears (**Figure 4.41**).

4. (Optional) To use a picture bullet, click the Picture button in the Bullets and Numbering dialog, then pick a bullet from the resulting Picture Bullet dialog. To use a different character bullet, click the Customize button in the Bullets and Numbering dialog, which brings up the Symbol dialog (Figure 4.10).

✔ Tip

■ If you click Import in the Picture Bullet dialog, you will be prompted to find a graphic on your hard disk or network. You can use any image you like, and PowerPoint will scale it to fit.

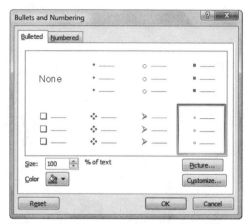

Figure 4.41 You can further refine your bulleted or numbered lists with the Bullets and Numbering dialog.

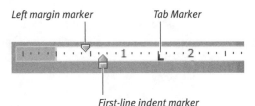

Left margin marker　　　*Tab Marker*

First-line indent marker

Figure 4.42 Use PowerPoint's ruler to set indents and tabs.

Setting Text and Bullet Tabs

PowerPoint allows you to set tabs within bulleted text boxes and free text boxes in much the same way that you could set tabs in a word processor. As with word processors, you'll set tabs using rulers and tab markers.

When you display PowerPoint's rulers and set the insertion point into a text box, you'll see a variety of markers on the ruler showing you the tabs and indents for the text box (**Figure 4.42**). The markers are as follows:

◆ **First-line indent marker** is useful mainly in free text boxes. It allows you to set a first-line indent. If you drag this marker to the left of the text indent marker, you'll create an outdent, where the first line hangs by itself to the left of the rest of the text.

◆ **Left margin marker** sets the left margin for the text within the text box. This marker is usually in the same position as the first-line indent marker.

◆ **Tab markers** allow you to set left, center, right, and decimal tabs.

To set and change text indents and tabs:

1. If it is not already visible, show PowerPoint's ruler by choosing View > Ruler.

   The ruler appears above the slide.

2. Click to set the insertion point in a text box where you want to set or change tabs or indents.

   The indent and tab markers for that line appear on the ruler.

3. To add a new tab, click the ruler.

   or

   To remove a tab from the ruler, drag it off the ruler.

   or

   To move tabs or indents, drag them left or right on the ruler.

   By default, PowerPoint puts a left tab on the ruler when you click.

4. (Optional) To change a tab on the ruler from one sort of tab to another, click the Open Paragraph Dialog Box button, then click the Tabs button in the resulting dialog. The Tabs dialog will appear, and you can set left, right, center, or decimal tabs.

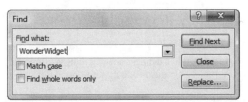

Figure 4.43 The Find dialog is also useful for replacing text; it turns into the Replace dialog if you click the Replace button.

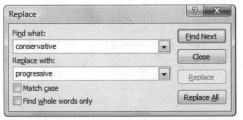

Figure 4.44 You'll use the Replace window to find and change text in your presentation.

Finding and Replacing Text

PowerPoint allows you to find and replace text on your slides, which is handy when Marketing tells you that they've decided to rename the SuperWidget to UltraWidget half an hour before your presentation.

To find text:

1. Choose Home > Editing > Find, or press Ctrl F.
   The Find dialog appears (**Figure 4.43**).

2. In the Find what field, enter the text you wish to find.

3. Click Find Next, or press Enter.
   PowerPoint finds the text.

To find and replace text:

1. Choose Home> Editing > Replace, or press Ctrl H.
   The Replace dialog appears (**Figure 4.44**).

2. In the Find what field, enter the text you wish to find.

3. In the Replace with field, enter the text you want to replace the found text.

4. (Optional) Choose either (or both) Match case and Find whole words only.

5. Click Replace to replace the first instance of the found text, or Replace All to replace the text throughout your presentation.

✔ Tip

- If you make a mistake when replacing text, you can use Undo to fix the mistake. Just press Ctrl Z or click the Undo button in the Quick Access Toolbar.

Checking Your Spelling

PowerPoint allows you check your spelling in two ways. By default, the program checks spelling as you type, and misspellings show up on your slides with red dotted underlines (**Figure 4.45**). Right-click on the underlined word to get a shortcut menu that includes possible replacements. Or you can check spelling manually.

To check spelling manually:

1. Choose Review > Proofing > Spelling (**Figure 4.46**), or press F7.

   The Spelling window appears (**Figure 4.47**).

2. Use the controls in the Spelling window to check your text.

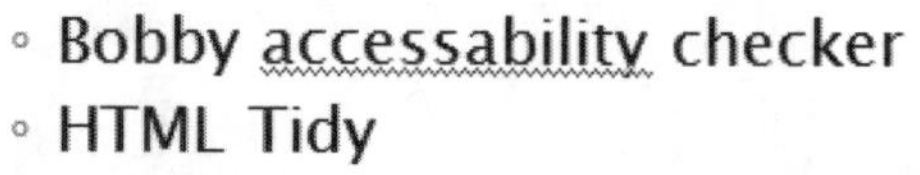

- Bobby accessability checker
- HTML Tidy

Figure 4.45 When dynamic spellchecking is turned on, PowerPoint flags suspect text with a dotted red underline.

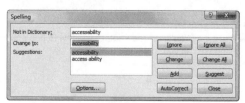

Figure 4.46 Click the Spelling button to run a manual spell check.

Figure 4.47 Use the controls in the Spelling window to check your spelling manually and to add new words to the spelling dictionary.

WORKING
WITH GRAPHICS

5

The text on your slides will usually carry the weight of your presentation, but the content can be greatly enhanced by the look of your slideshow. Much of that look is provided by the theme you select for your presentation. But graphics on the slide can also add zing to a professional-looking presentation, and often they contribute a significant part of the content of the presentation, as well.

In this chapter, you'll learn how to use PowerPoint—with the help of other graphics programs—to add and enhance graphics for your slides.

Placing Graphics and Shapes

The graphics on your slides will be one of three types: the first two are *imported graphics*, which include photographs and drawings from other graphic programs and Office 2007's clip art; and *shapes*, which are simple vector graphics that you can create within PowerPoint. PowerPoint's shapes can be scaled and manipulated with no loss of resolution. The third kind of graphic, *SmartArt*, will be covered in Chapter 6.

PowerPoint's repertoire of shapes is quite extensive, and you can use one or more of them to create diagrams or otherwise illustrate your concepts.

To insert a picture:

1. In the Normal View pane, click to select the thumbnail of the slide you want to put the graphic on.

2. If the layout on the slide includes a content box, click the Insert Picture from File icon in the content box (**Figure 5.1**).

   or

   If the layout does not have a content box, choose Insert > Illustrations > Picture (**Figure 5.2**).

   The Insert Picture dialog appears. Navigate to the picture you want, select it in the dialog, and click Open.

   The picture appears on your slide (**Figure 5.3**).

   or

   Open the folder on the Windows desktop that contains the picture file, then drag the icon for that file into the PowerPoint window.

   The picture appears on your slide.

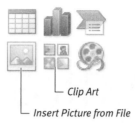

Clip Art

Insert Picture from File

Figure 5.1 Insert pictures in content boxes by clicking the Insert Picture from File icon.

Figure 5.2 If your slide doesn't have a content box, use the Picture button on the Ribbon's Insert tab.

My Life as a Cat

The Greatest Story Ever Told

Figure 5.3 The picture of Pixel, my cat, is placed on the presentation slide. As you can see, he thinks rather highly of himself.

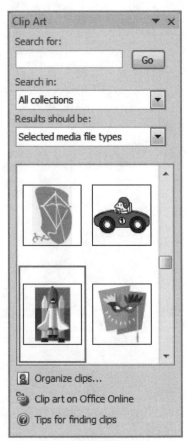

Figure 5.4 You can search for clip art on your computer or on Microsoft's Web site with the Clip Art task pane.

✔ Tips

- You can often drag and drop graphic files into a PowerPoint slide from other applications. This doesn't always function correctly, so try it and see if it works.

- PowerPoint can import a wide range of graphic file formats, including TIFF, JPEG, GIF, PNG, PICT (old Macintosh graphic format), BMP (Windows bitmapped image format), and more.

- If you have an image with an alpha channel, meaning it has transparent areas, you'll be much happier if you convert it to PNG format before you bring it into PowerPoint. TIFF files with transparency often do not work well in PowerPoint.

- You can almost always copy a graphic in another application, switch to PowerPoint, and paste the graphic into the slide.

To insert clip art:

1. Select the thumbnail of the slide you want to put the graphic on.

2. If the layout on the slide includes a content box, click the Clip Art icon in the content box (Figure 5.1).

   or

   If the layout does not have a content box, choose Insert > Illustrations > Clip Art (Figure 5.2).

   The Clip Art task pane appears (**Figure 5.4**).

   This task pane contains the Clip Organizer.

   continues on next page

3. Type a search term into the Search for text field and click the Go button.

The first time you do this, PowerPoint pops up a dialog asking you if you want to include search results from Microsoft's huge online repository of clip art. Assuming you have an always-on Internet connection, click Yes; you'll get a better, more diverse range of results.

PowerPoint searches the available clip art and displays items that match your search text.

4. Scroll through the search results until you find the one you want, then double-click it.

The clip art appears on your slide.

Using Clip Art Packages

If you're looking for inexpensive ways to improve the graphics on your slides, many packages of clip art are available. These usually come on a series of CD-ROMs (or sometimes on DVD-ROMs, which hold much more data), and are usually licensed as royalty free, which means that you can use them as you want in your presentations, with no further payments needed to the photographers or artists who created the images. Clip art packages can consist of photographs, vector artwork, bitmapped artwork, or sometimes even fonts.

For example, many of the photographic images in this book were taken from Nova Development's Photo-Objects 150,000 package (www.novadevelopment.com). The program offers an image browser that lets you enter keywords to find the photos that you need, then you can export them in a variety of formats (for PowerPoint, PNG with Transparency works best).

There are many other places to find good clip art, especially online, where there are far too many to list. Do a Google search for "royalty free" images.

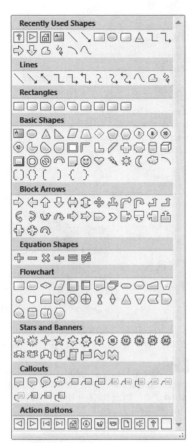

Figure 5.5 The Shapes gallery contains more than a hundred drawing shapes, ready for you to place on your slides.

Figure 5.6 Once a shape is selected on your slide, you can modify it in many ways, including resizing it, changing its fill color, rotating it, and so on.

To place PowerPoint shapes:

1. Select the slide you want to put the shape on.

2. From the Insert > Illustrations > Shapes gallery in the toolbar, choose the shape that you want (**Figure 5.5**).

   The gallery is broken up into types, so you can find a shape easily.

3. The cursor turns into a crosshair.

4. Click and drag the cursor on the slide to draw the shape onto the slide.

   If you hold down the Shift key when drawing the shape, it will draw proportionately, so the horizontal and vertical dimensions are equal. This is especially useful when you are drawing circular or square shapes.

   The shape appears on the slide (**Figure 5.6**). It is selected, so you can modify it.

✔ Tip

- Once you place a shape, you cannot change it to a different kind of shape. For example, you can't convert a rectangle into a circle.

To delete graphics or shapes:

- To delete a shape or imported graphic, select it and press Backspace or Delete.

Resizing and Cropping Graphics

Once you have placed your image into PowerPoint, you will usually have to resize it in some way. That can mean scaling it (making it bigger or smaller) or cropping it (trimming the image to only the part you want). You can do both right in PowerPoint.

Scaling graphics

You can scale graphics in one of two ways: you can drag the graphic object's selection handles, or you can use the Size group or Size and Position dialog in the Drawing Tools or Picture Tools contextual tab (**Figure 5.7**). The Size and Position dialog gives you the most precise control.

To resize objects using selection handles:

1. Select the image on your slide.

   Selection handles appear around the image (**Figure 5.8**).

2. Click and drag one of the handles to resize the object.

3. After you resize the object to your liking, it will probably not be in the correct position on the slide. Drag it to a position more to your liking.

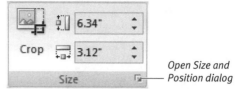

Open Size and Position dialog

Figure 5.7 This group is from the Picture Tools contextual tab. The Size group on the Drawing Tools contextual tab is similar, except that it lacks the Crop tool.

Figure 5.8 When you select an image, selection handles appear around it. Drag the selection handles at the edges of an image to resize it.

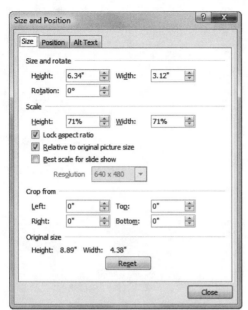

Figure 5.9 You can also use the Size and Position dialog to resize objects in more precise increments than you can by dragging selection handles.

To resize objects with the Size group or Size dialog:

1. Select the image on your slide.

2. Use the Height and Width controls in the Size group of the Picture Tools or Drawing Tools contextual tab to enter a new size (Figure 5.7).

   You can type a figure into the Width or Height box, or you can use the arrow buttons to make small changes.

   When you're happy with your changes, you're done.

3. (Optional) If you want more control, click the Size dialog button at the lower-right corner of the Size group.

   The Size and Position dialog appears (**Figure 5.9**).

4. (Optional) Use the controls in this dialog to set the size, rotation, and scaling of the image.

   For pictures (but not for shapes) the Crop from section is active, allowing you to crop the picture numerically.

5. Click Close when you are done.

✔ Tips

- The Original size section of the Size and Position dialog shows the beginning size of the graphic, so you have an idea of how different your changes are from the original. The Reset button in this section undoes all of your changes, but it is only available for pictures, not for drawn shapes.

- You can use the Position tab of the Size and Position dialog to precisely position an object on the slide.

RESIZING AND CROPPING GRAPHICS

Cropping pictures

When you crop a picture, you effectively strip away all but the parts of the picture you want. Cropping is useful when you like part of a picture, but not all of it, and you want to focus on just the important or relevant portion. You can only crop pictures, not shapes.

To crop a picture:

1. Select the picture you want to crop.

2. Choose Picture Tools > Format > Size > Crop (Figure 5.7).

   Crop handles appear at the edges of the picture, and the cursor turns into the crop symbol.

3. Drag one or more of the crop handles to exclude part of the picture.

4. Click off the picture to lock in your change.

✔ Tip

- Cropping a picture only hides the portion of the picture that appears to be removed; it doesn't actually edit the picture and remove those pixels. If you change your mind at a later date, you can use the Crop tool again and resize the crop area, in effect "uncropping" the picture.

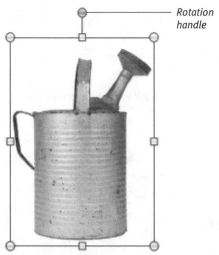

Rotation handle

Figure 5.10 Click and drag the object's rotation handle to free rotate it.

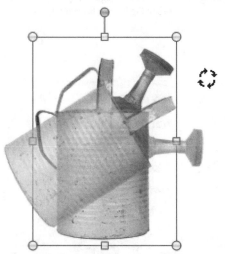

Figure 5.11 As you rotate the object, the ghost image shows you what will happen when you release the mouse button.

Rotating and Flipping Graphic Objects

PowerPoint allows you to rotate objects on the slide canvas. You rotate objects by dragging the object's rotation handle (this is called free rotation), or using the Rotation field in the Size and Position dialog. You can also flip objects around their horizontal or vertical axes. Objects that have text inside them (see "Placing Text Within Shapes," later in this chapter) use a different technique to flip them.

To free-rotate objects:

1. Select the object you want to rotate.

   The object's selection handles appear. The top handle (the one with the green dot) is the *rotation handle* (**Figure 5.10**).

2. Click and drag the object's rotation handle.

   The cursor changes to four short curved lines with an arrow at one end. As you rotate the object, you get a ghost image of the object, which tells you how far the rotation has gone (**Figure 5.11**).

3. Release the mouse button.

To rotate using the Size and Position dialog:

1. Select the object you want to rotate.

2. Right-click on the object, then choose Size and Position from the shortcut menu. The Size and Position dialog appears.

3. In the Size and rotate section (**Figure 5.12**), click the up or down buttons next to the Rotation field.

   or

   Type a value into the Rotation field and press the Tab key.

   The object rotates.

✔ Tip

■ When you need to make small or precise changes, you can often get better results by typing a value into the rotation field, rather than using the object's rotation handle.

To flip objects:

1. Select the object you want to flip.

   It can be a drawing shape or a picture.

2. Choose Drawing Tools > Format > Arrange > Rotate, then choose Flip Vertical or Flip Horizontal from the pop-up menu (**Figure 5.13**).

   or

   Choose Picture Tools > Format > Arrange > Rotate, then choose Flip Vertical or Flip Horizontal from the pop-up menu.

   The object flips as you command (**Figure 5.14**).

✔ Tip

■ When you flip an object that contains text, PowerPoint is smart enough not to flip the text as well, which would make it unreadable.

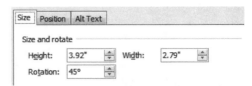

Figure 5.12 The Size and Position dialog gives you precise rotation control in degrees.

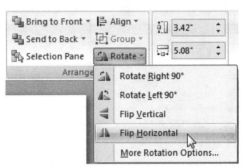

Figure 5.13 From the Rotate pop-up menu, use the Flip menu choices to flip images horizontally or vertically.

Figure 5.14 After the flip, the quote balloon points in a different direction, but the text is still readable.

Figure 5.15 The Align menu lets you arrange objects on the slide in relation to each other, or to the slide as a whole.

Table 5.1

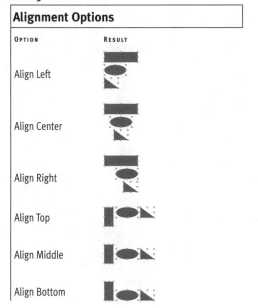

Alignment Options	
OPTION	RESULT
Align Left	
Align Center	
Align Right	
Align Top	
Align Middle	
Align Bottom	

Aligning and Distributing Objects

PowerPoint provides commands that make it easy to arrange multiple objects so that they all line up with their edges or centers along the same line. You can also distribute objects so that they are arranged, either horizontally or vertically, with equal space between them.

With either alignment or distribution, you can choose to have the objects move relative to each other, or relative to the slide.

To align objects:

1. Select the objects that you want to align.

2. Depending on if you have selected a picture or a drawing, choose Picture Tools or Drawing Tools, then Format > Arrange > Align, then choose the kind of alignment you want from the pop-up menu (**Figure 5.15**). Your choices are Align Left, Align Center, Align Right, Align Top, Align Middle, and Align Bottom. See **Table 5.1** to see how the different alignments work.

3. (Optional) If you want the objects to be aligned to each other, choose Align Selected Objects from the Align pop-up menu. If you want the objects to be aligned to the whole slide, choose Align to Slide.

To distribute objects:

1. Select the objects that you wish to distribute.

2. Depending on if you have selected a picture or a drawing, choose Picture Tools or Drawing Tools, then Format > Arrange > Align, then choose the kind of alignment you want from the pop-up menu. Your choices are Distribute Horizontally or Distribute Vertically.

   See **Table 5.2** to see how the different distributions work.

3. (Optional) If you want the objects to be aligned to each other, choose Align Selected Objects from the Align pop-up menu. If you want the objects to be aligned to the whole slide, choose Align to Slide.

Table 5.2

Distribution Options		
OPTION	BEFORE COMMAND	RESULT
Distribute Horizontally		
Distribute Vertically		

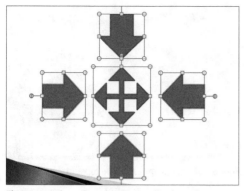

Figure 5.16 These five objects are all selected; you can tell because all of their selection handles are visible.

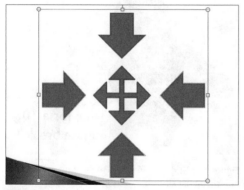

Figure 5.17 After grouping, there is only one set of selection handles.

Grouping Objects

If you have several graphic objects, you might find it easier to work with them as a *group*. You can move the group on the slide or copy and paste it between slides, which is much easier than selecting multiple objects. Grouping objects also preserves their positions relative to one another.

To group objects:

1. Select the objects you want to group (**Figure 5.16**).

2. Choose Drawing Tools or Picture Tools > Format > Arrange > Group, or press Ctrl G.

   The objects group, and there is now one set of selection handles for the group (**Figure 5.17**).

✔ Tip

- You can free-rotate grouped objects by clicking and grabbing on the grouped objects' rotation handle.

To ungroup objects:

1. Select the group.

2. Choose Drawing Tools or Picture Tools > Format > Arrange > Ungroup.

   The objects ungroup.

Using Rulers and Gridlines

In order to precisely place objects on the slide canvas, PowerPoint provides two tools: rulers and gridlines. Rulers appear at the top and left edges of the slide canvas, and the gridlines overlay the entire slide. Gridlines do not appear when you play the presentation.

To toggle rulers on and off:

1. Choose View > Show/Hide > Ruler.

   The rulers appear above and to the left of the slide area (**Figure 5.18**).

2. Choose View > Show/Hide > Ruler again to hide the rulers.

✔ Tip

■ If you don't see the vertical ruler, you may need to turn it on in PowerPoint's preferences. Choose Office Button > PowerPoint Options, then in the resulting dialog, click the Advanced category. In the Display section, select Show vertical ruler. Then click OK to dismiss the Options dialog.

To turn on the gridlines:

1. Choose View > Show/Hide > Gridlines.

   The gridlines appear in the slide area (**Figure 5.19**).

   You can use the gridlines to make sure that objects on the slide are aligned properly, or to make sure that objects are the same distance apart.

2. Choose View > Show/Hide > Gridlines again to hide the grid.

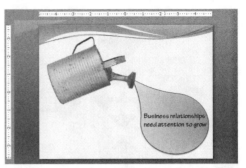

Figure 5.18 Rulers appear at the top and left edges of the slide canvas.

Figure 5.19 Gridlines appear over all of the text and objects on the slide.

Figure 5.20 The picture of the hapless couple is in front of the title text and the image of the television.

Figure 5.21 After sending the image backward, the benighted couch potatoes appear to be trapped inside the television.

Layering Graphics

When you place objects on slides, you can think of each object as being in its own layer on the slide. For example, if you have five objects on a slide, you have six layers: one layer for each object, plus the slide background, which is defined in the template. You can move each of these layers forward and back. The exception is the slide background, the layer furthest back, which can't be brought forward.

Any text boxes that are part of the slide, such as the title box and the content box (with or without bulleted text), can be layered like any other object.

To layer slide objects:

1. Select a slide object that you want to move forward or backward in the slide layers (**Figure 5.20**).

2. To send the object to the back of the layers, choose Drawing Tools or Picture Tools > Format > Arrange > Send to Back.

   or

   To move the object back in the layers, choose Drawing Tools or Picture Tools > Format > Arrange > Send Backwards. This moves the object one layer back.

   or

   To bring the object to the front, choose Drawing Tools or Picture Tools > Format > Arrange > Bring to Front.

   or

   To move the object forward in the layers, choose Drawing Tools or Picture Tools > Format > Arrange > Bring Forward. This moves the object one layer forward.

   The object moves as you command.

3. Drag the still-selected object to position it as you want with the other layers (**Figure 5.21**).

   You can also resize the object to get a more pleasing effect.

Using Color, Texture, and Gradient Fills

You can fill shapes created in PowerPoint with solid colors, color gradients, one of the built-in *textures* (an image designed to tile smoothly inside a shape) or an image (see "Placing Images within Objects"). A *color* fill replaces the interior of the object with a solid color, picked from the colors palette. A *gradient fill* creates a smooth blend from one color that you set to a second color. You can fill any of the drawing objects created in the PowerPoint Shapes gallery, and you can also fill the shapes (bars, columns, pie slices, and so on) in PowerPoint charts. You use the Drawing Tools > Format > Shape Styles group to apply fills to shapes (**Figure 5.22**).

You might find it easier to use one of PowerPoint's built-in shape styles, which are 42 preset solid fills with contrasting text and border colors. You can apply a shape style with a click.

To fill a shape with a shape style:

1. Select the shape you want to fill.

2. Choose a style from the Drawing Tools > Format > Shape Styles gallery.

   or

   To see all the styles, click the gallery's More button.

   The gallery opens (**Figure 5.23**). Click on a style to select it.

   The shape fills with the style (**Figure 5.24**).

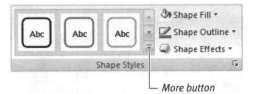

— More button

Figure 5.22 Use the Shape Styles gallery to easily add fills to objects.

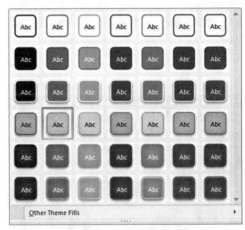

Figure 5.23 There are a wide variety of preset fills.

Figure 5.24 I applied a different shape style to each of these two objects.

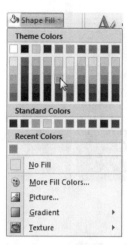

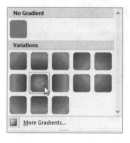

Figure 5.25 Pick a color from the Shape Fill gallery.

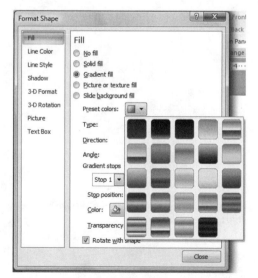

Figure 5.26 The Gradient gallery has many variations from which to choose.

Figure 5.27 If you want more gradient choices, you'll find them in the Format Shape dialog.

To fill a shape with a solid color:

1. Select the shape you want to fill.

2. Choose a color from the Drawing Tools > Format > Shape Styles > Shape Fill gallery (**Figure 5.25**).

   As you roll over the colors, the shape changes to match in a live preview. When you click, the color is applied.

To fill a shape with a gradient:

1. Select the shape you want to fill.

2. Choose from the Drawing Tools > Format > Shape Styles > Shape Fill > Gradient gallery (**Figure 5.26**).

   The shape fills with the selected gradient fill. If you're happy with the effect, you're done.

3. (Optional) If you want more gradient choices, choose More Gradients from the bottom of the gradient gallery.

   The Format Shape dialog appears.

4. (Optional) Choose a gradient from the Preset colors pop-up menu (**Figure 5.27**).

   or

   Use the controls in the dialog to customize the gradient as you like.

5. (Optional) Click Close.

   The shape is filled with the gradient (**Figure 5.28**).

Figure 5.28 This object is filled with a smooth gradient from dark to light to dark again.

To fill a shape with a texture:

1. Select the shape you want to fill.

2. Choose from the Drawing Tools > Format > Shape Styles > Shape Fill > Texture gallery (**Figure 5.29**).

   The shape fills with the selected texture (**Figure 5.30**).

✔ Tip

■ Choosing More Textures from the Texture gallery brings up the Format Shape dialog, which allows you to load a picture or clip art and use it as a texture.

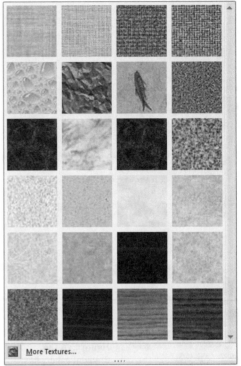

Figure 5.29 Use the Texture gallery for a different sort of fill for your shapes.

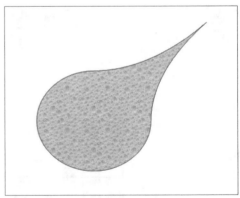

Figure 5.30 This teardrop shape is filled with a water drop texture.

Figure 5.31 This text is embedded in the shape, moves with the shape, and rewraps as the shape is resized.

Placing Text Within Shapes

PowerPoint allows you the ability to place text directly within shapes you've created in PowerPoint. Shapes can have any kind of color, gradient, or image fill, and the text that you add will be overlaid on the fill. Text inside the shape rewraps as you resize the shape.

To add text to a shape:

1. Using Insert > Illustrations > Shapes, place a shape on the slide you're working with.

2. Resize the shape to your liking, and add a color, gradient, or image fill as needed.

3. Right-click in the middle of the shape, then choose Edit Text from the shortcut menu. An insertion point will appear, centered in the shape.

4. Type the text you want in the shape (**Figure 5.31**).

5. (Optional) Select and right-click the text, then change the font, font size, or other formatting from the mini toolbar.

Placing Images Within Objects

In a similar manner to color and gradient fills, you can fill shapes in PowerPoint with images. You can use any kind of image that PowerPoint can import.

To fill a shape with an image:

1. Select the shape you want to fill.

2. Choose Drawing Tools > Format > Shape Styles > Shape Fill > Picture.

   The Insert Picture dialog appears.

3. Navigate to and select the picture you want inside the shape, then click Open.

   The image appears inside the shape (**Figure 5.32**).

✔ Tip

■ Lines are a kind of shape, but you can't fill them with an image, even if you change their weight so that they are very thick. Consider using rectangle shapes instead.

Figure 5.32 Images inside shapes can be interesting, as with this beach scene inside the sun shape.

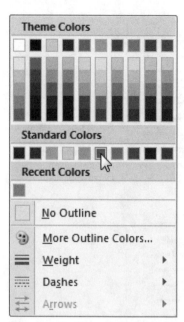

Figure 5.33 The Shape Outline gallery lets you change the color, thickness, or line style of the outline.

Modifying Shape and Picture Outlines

The borders of a shape or picture are delineated in PowerPoint by the *outline*, which is the line around the object. PowerPoint allows you to set the line style, line thickness, and line color for shapes. If you prefer, you can have no outline around an object. For line shapes, you can also set a graphic (such as an arrowhead or a circle) for the line's endpoints.

PowerPoint has different contextual tabs on the Ribbon for pictures and shapes, which makes the controls for outlining pictures and shapes slightly different. For pictures, you'll find them at Picture Tools > Format > Picture Styles > Picture Border. For shapes, you'll find them at Drawing Tools > Format > Shape Styles > Shape Outline. Despite their different locations and names, picture borders and shape outlines work the same. For the purposes of the example here, we'll see how to change the outline of a shape.

There is another gallery in the Picture Styles group, the Picture Styles, which we'll discuss in "Applying Picture Styles," later in this chapter.

To set the outline for an object:

1. Select the object for which you want to set the outline.

2. Choose Drawing Tools > Format > Shape Styles > Shape Outline. The Shape Outline gallery appears (**Figure 5.33**).

continues on next page

3. Choose one or more of the following:

▲ To change the color of the outline, choose one of the color swatches under Theme Colors, Standard Colors, or Recent Colors.

▲ To remove the outline, choose No Outline.

▲ If you want a color that isn't in the color swatches, choose More Outline Colors. The Colors dialog appears, with your choice of two color pickers in it. Choose a color, then click OK.

▲ To change the thickness of the outline, make a selection from the Weight fly-out menu (**Figure 5.34**).

▲ To change the style of the outline, from a solid line to different sorts of dashes, make a selection from the Dashes fly-out menu (**Figure 5.35**).

▲ If the shape you are changing is a line, the Arrows fly-out menu will be available (**Figure 5.36**). Make a choice from this menu if you want to add or change the endpoints of a line.

The shape's outline changes as you command (**Figure 5.37**).

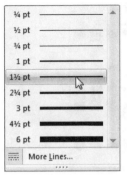

Figure 5.34 The Weight gallery lets you change the thickness of the outline in small increments.

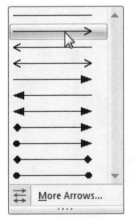

Figure 5.35 The Dashes gallery gives you a variety of line styles.

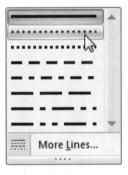

Figure 5.36 If the selected shape is a line, you can choose whether or not it has arrows on one end, both ends, and you have control over the arrowhead style.

Figure 5.37 This image uses a dashed, fairly thick outline.

Figure 5.38 The Picture Tools contextual tab.

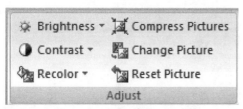

Figure 5.39 The Adjust group allows you to change the brightness, contrast, and other image parameters.

Modifying Pictures and Clip Art

Sometimes pictures and clip art look pretty much the way you want them to when you place them on your slides. Other times, they don't give you 100% of the effect that you would prefer. Though PowerPoint is certainly no photo editing program, it does allow you to make some changes to your pictures, such as changing the brightness and contrast and overlaying a color hue. Still, if you want to make serious changes or touch ups to your pictures, do them in a real photo editing program, such as Adobe Photoshop or Photoshop Elements, before you bring them into PowerPoint.

When you select a picture or clip art, the Picture Tools contextual tab appears on the Ribbon with a Format subtab (**Figure 5.38**). You'll use the Adjust group (**Figure 5.39**) to make your changes. **Table 5.3** runs down the controls in this group.

Table 5.3

Picture Adjustment Tools	
BUTTON	**DESCRIPTION**
Brightness	Displays a gallery that allows you to change the picture's brightness in 10% increments, from 40% dimmer to 40% brighter.
Contrast	Displays a gallery that adjusts the picture's contrast in 10% increments, from 40% less contrast to 40% greater contrast.
Recolor	Displays a gallery with color overlays, such as grayscale, CPS, and duotones.
Compress Pictures	Allows you to compress the picture, reducing its file size.
Change Picture	Allows you to replace the current picture with a different picture.
Reset Picture	Restores the image to its original state.

To adjust a picture or clip art image:

1. Select the picture or clip art you want to modify.

The Picture Tools contextual tab appears in the Ribbon.

2. From the Picture Tools > Format > Adjust group, click the button for the modification that you want.

If you chose Brightness, Contrast, or Recolor, a gallery appears. Choose the effect you want from the gallery. In this example, we're using the Brightness gallery (**Figure 5.40**).

The modification is applied to the picture (**Figure 5.41**).

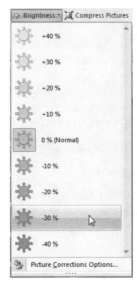

Figure 5.40 Use the Brightness gallery to change the look of the picture.

Figure 5.41 This illustration of a beach scene (top) looks more ominous with the brightness turned down (bottom).

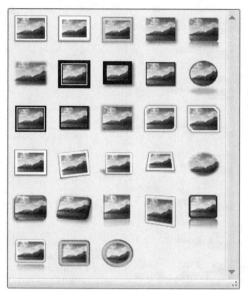

Figure 5.42 The Picture Styles gallery contains many useful framing effects for your pictures.

Figure 5.43 This picture style vignetted the picture into a rounded rectangle, added a drop shadow, and tilted the picture in perspective. Not bad for a single click.

Applying Picture Styles

Picture styles are a selection of picture treatments you can apply to pictures and clip art that provide a variety of preset effects to the image, such as a frame, a vignette, soft edges, and even reflection and 3-D rotation effects.

To apply a picture style:

1. Select the picture or clip art you want to modify.

   The Picture Tools contextual tab appears in the Ribbon.

2. From the Picture Tools > Format > Picture Styles group, choose a picture style from the gallery.

   or

   To see all the preset Picture styles, click the More button at the lower-right corner of the Picture Styles gallery.

   The gallery appears (**Figure 5.42**).

3. Select a style from the gallery.

   The selected image takes on the style you chose (**Figure 5.43**).

Applying Picture and Shape Effects

Effects are vital tools in PowerPoint because they dress up objects on your slides, giving them an appearance of depth, or making them stand out from other elements on the slide. Some common examples of effects are drop shadows and glows. New effects in PowerPoint 2007 include reflections, beveling, and 3-D rotations.

PowerPoint, using the Picture Tools and Drawing Tools contextual tabs, provides similar, but not identical, effects capabilities for pictures and vector illustrations such as shapes.

To apply an effect to a picture:

1. Select the picture to which you want to add the effect.

2. Choose Picture Tools > Format > Picture Styles > Picture Effects.

    As you can see, this menu provides seven effects categories from which to choose (**Figure 5.44**).

3. Choose one of the effects categories, and a gallery will appear.

    This example uses the Reflection category (**Figure 5.45**).

4. Select one of the effects in the gallery you displayed.

    The effect is applied to the object (**Figure 5.46**).

Figure 5.44 The Picture Effects menu provides seven effects galleries for your pictures.

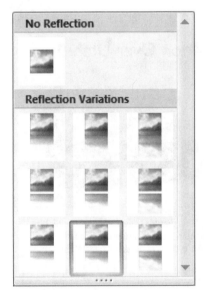

Figure 5.45 This Reflection gallery shows you some of the many options available.

Figure 5.46 The result of the Reflection effect appears below the image, then fades away smoothly.

Figure 5.47 The Shape Effects menu provides seven effects galleries for your shapes.

To apply an effect to a shape:

1. Select the shape to which you want to add the effect.

2. Choose Drawing Tools > Format > Shape Styles > Shape Effects.

   This menu provides seven effects categories from which to choose (**Figure 5.47**).

3. Choose one of the effects categories, and a gallery will appear.

4. Select one of the effects in the gallery you displayed.

   The effect is applied to the object.

✔ Tips

- If you have more than one object with a drop shadow, it's usually a good idea to give all the objects the same shadow values.

- You can copy and paste effects settings from one object to another by selecting the first object, choosing Home > Clipboard > Format Painter, and clicking on the second object. Be aware that this also copies and pastes the border, fill, and opacity of the object.

APPLYING PICTURE AND SHAPE EFFECTS

Using WordArt

WordArt is a feature that allows you to take text and format it in graphically interesting ways. Office 2007 actually provides two entirely different things, and calls them *both* WordArt (thanks for the confusion, Microsoft!).

The first sort of WordArt is available in both PowerPoint and Word, and it lets you apply bevels, shadows, and text transformations to regular text. This creates decorative text that can be used as headline and accent text (**Figure 5.48**).

The second kind of WordArt is only available in Word, but it can be copied and pasted into PowerPoint. This kind of WordArt comes into PowerPoint as a vector image, so you can still make changes to it using the Drawing Tools contextual tab, but the text is still editable (**Figure 5.49**).

You can use WordArt text of either kind as headlines for slides, or as additional graphic touches anywhere on the slide canvas.

Figure 5.48 These are only some of the WordArt effects available within PowerPoint.

Figure 5.49 This WordArt was created in Microsoft Word, then copied and pasted into PowerPoint as a vector drawing.

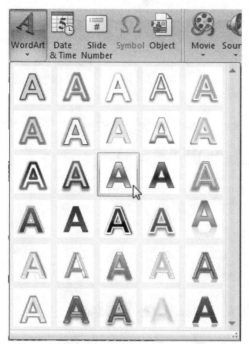

Figure 5.50 Pick a style from the WordArt gallery.

Figure 5.51 Replace the placeholder text for the WordArt.

To create WordArt in PowerPoint:

1. Display the slide on which you want the WordArt.

2. Choose Insert > Text > WordArt, then pick a style from the WordArt gallery (**Figure 5.50**).

   A text box appears on the slide, with the "Your Text Here" placeholder text selected and ready for you to replace it (**Figure 5.51**).

3. Type the text you want, then click anywhere else on the slide.

   The text is styled as WordArt.

✔ Tip

■ You can make further changes to this kind of WordArt by selecting it and using the tools in Drawing Tools > Format > WordArt Styles. There are some wild styles here, especially in the Text Effects pop-up menu.

To create and import WordArt from Word:

1. Create a blank Word 2007 document, type in the text you want to make into WordArt, then select that text.

2. Choose Insert > Text > WordArt. The WordArt gallery appears (**Figure 5.52**).

3. Click one of the styles to select it. The Edit WordArt Text dialog appears with your text in it (**Figure 5.53**).

4. In the Edit WordArt Text dialog, you can choose to change the font, font size, and style the text as bold or italic.

5. Click OK. The WordArt image appears in your Word document. The image is already selected.

6. Choose Home > Clipboard > Copy, or press Ctrl C.

7. Switch to PowerPoint.

8. Display the destination slide.

9. Choose Home > Clipboard > Paste, or press Ctrl V. The WordArt image appears on your PowerPoint slide.

10. The WordArt image will probably appear too small and will need to be resized to fit properly on the slide.

✔ Tip

- WordArt images from Word can be manipulated in many, but not all, of the ways that you would manipulate other images in PowerPoint. You can scale, flip, rotate, and add effects in PowerPoint, but you can't change the color fill of the lettering. You can change the outline color and style, but all that will be affected will be a box around the image, not the edges of the letters in the image, which makes this fairly useless.

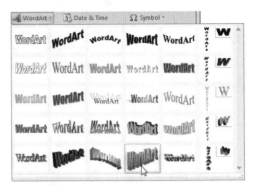

Figure 5.52 The WordArt gallery in Word has an entirely different set of choices.

Figure 5.53 Use this dialog to edit the text for your WordArt.

ADDING SMARTART

In Chapter 5, we saw how to work with graphics, including images from your hard drive and clip art. But there's another kind of graphic that is really important to many presentations, and that would be the diagram. A good diagram can easily take the place of a hundred words, and can be understood by your audience at a glance.

Office 2007 completely revamps the way that you create diagrams, providing an easy-to-use diagramming feature called *SmartArt*. You can insert SmartArt in PowerPoint 2007, Word 2007, Excel 2007, and Outlook 2007. Once you create a SmartArt graphic, you can copy and paste it into documents from other programs as well.

One of the great things about SmartArt is that it provides a large prebuilt library of diagrams, and those diagrams automatically size, position, and most importantly, re-color themselves according to the design theme you've applied to your presentation. This automatic color coordination with the rest of your presentation is a tremendous timesaver.

You have your choice of converting bulleted text into a SmartArt diagram, or simply inserting SmartArt into a slide and adding text to it. In this chapter, you'll see how to create and use SmartArt in your presentations.

Inserting and Deleting SmartArt

A SmartArt diagram consists of two parts. The diagram is made up of one or more graphic shapes, usually with text in each shape. The text can be entered directly in each shape, but it's much easier to add it in the *text pane*, which is attached to the SmartArt when you create or modify it (**Figure 6.1**).

You can put SmartArt on any slide, but it's a little easier to put it on slides with content boxes. You can also convert bulleted text in a content box to SmartArt, which is handy when you change your mind about a slide and decide you would prefer to show it as a diagram instead of plain text.

If you don't want the SmartArt after all, it's easy to get rid of it.

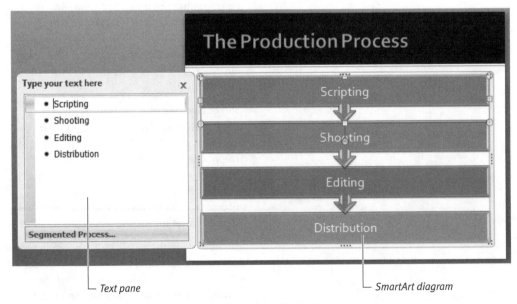

Text pane
SmartArt diagram

Figure 6.1 You can add text either to the SmartArt diagram itself, or in the text pane.

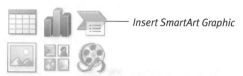

Figure 6.2 In layouts with content boxes, just click the Insert SmartArt Graphic button.

To insert SmartArt directly on a slide:

1. Display the slide where you want the SmartArt.

2. If the slide layout has a content box, click the Insert SmartArt Graphic icon (**Figure 6.2**).

   or

   If the slide layout does not have a content box, choose Insert > Illustrations > SmartArt.

   The Choose a SmartArt Graphic dialog appears (**Figure 6.3**). This dialog has three panes: the category list, the layouts, and the description.

3. In the category list, All is selected by default, showing you all of the different SmartArt varieties in a scrolling layout list. If you prefer, click one of the other categories to see layouts from just that category.

   It's possible to have more SmartArt categories than you see in Figure 6.3, if you have downloaded additional SmartArt from Microsoft or a third-party.

   continues on next page

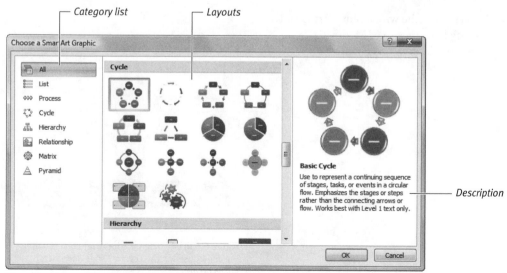

Figure 6.3 You use this dialog to insert all SmartArt.

4. In the middle pane, select the SmartArt layout that you want.

The description pane shows details about the selected layout (**Figure 6.4**). Since the text pane of the SmartArt can contain multiple levels of bulleted text, the description often tells you where each level of the text will go on the diagram.

5. Click OK.

The SmartArt diagram appears on the slide, with the text pane displayed, ready for you to enter text.

6. Enter text in the text pane as you would any bulleted text.

Click to replace the placeholder text that PowerPoint puts in the text pane, then type your text. Press Enter to create a new entry (for Level 1 text, this creates a new shape in the diagram). Press the Tab key to indent text to Level 2 (**Figure 6.5**).

7. When you're done, click elsewhere on the slide to dismiss the text pane and review your new SmartArt diagram (**Figure 6.6**).

✔ Tip

■ If you choose the wrong SmartArt layout, it's easy to change. See "Modifying SmartArt," later in this chapter.

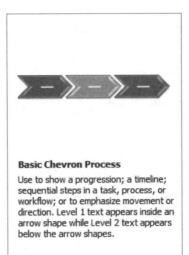

Basic Chevron Process

Use to show a progression; a timeline; sequential steps in a task, process, or workflow; or to emphasize movement or direction. Level 1 text appears inside an arrow shape while Level 2 text appears below the arrow shapes.

Figure 6.4 The description pane of the Choose a SmartArt Graphic dialog gives you useful information about the best way to use that particular SmartArt layout, and also about how you should use Level 1 and Level 2 text.

Figure 6.5 This text pane shows both Level 1 and Level 2 text, in bulleted form.

Figure 6.6 In this diagram, the Level 1 text is within the chevrons, and the Level 2 text is underneath each chevron.

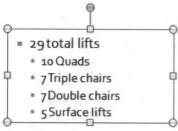

Figure 6.7 Bulleted text, ready to be turned into SmartArt.

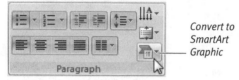

Convert to SmartArt Graphic

Figure 6.8 The Paragraph group lets you convert bulleted text to SmartArt.

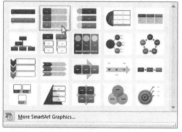

Figure 6.9 This gallery gives you some of the most appropriate SmartArt layouts for bulleted text.

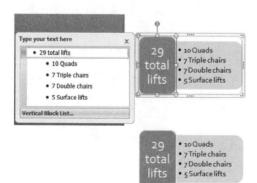

Figure 6.10 The completed SmartArt, selected with the text pane showing (top) and the finished product (bottom).

To convert bulleted text into SmartArt:

1. Select the bulleted text you would like to turn into SmartArt (**Figure 6.7**).

    It doesn't matter if you select the text or the whole text box that surrounds it.

2. Choose Home > Paragraph > Convert to SmartArt Graphic (**Figure 6.8**).

    A gallery of SmartArt graphics appears (**Figure 6.9**).

3. Choose a layout from the gallery.

    As you move your mouse cursor over the different layouts, PowerPoint shows you a live preview of what the new SmartArt graphic will look like on the slide.

4. Click to select a layout.

    The bulleted text turns into the new SmartArt, and the text pane is filled with the bulleted text, in case you want to edit it (**Figure 6.10**).

To delete SmartArt:

1. Select the SmartArt on your slide.

2. Press Backspace or Delete.

    The SmartArt disappears.

✔ Tip

■ Of course, you can also cut, copy, and paste a SmartArt graphic, just like any other object in PowerPoint.

Working with the Text Pane

The text pane is useful, but sometimes it gets in the way. After you have entered your initial text, you usually don't need to make much in the way of changes, and the text pane, extending as it does to the left of the slide, can often obscure the slide thumbnails in the Normal View pane.

The first step in changing the text pane is to realize that even though it looks as though it is stuck to the left side of the SmartArt graphic, it really isn't. It's a floating window, and you can deal with that window the way you would any other window, including closing it by clicking in the X in its upper-right corner; growing and shrinking it by dragging any edge or the lower-right corner; moving it anywhere on your screen, even outside the PowerPoint window, by dragging the text pane's title bar (where it says "Type your text here").

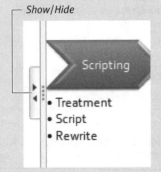

When you close the text pane, you can get it back in two ways. You can click the Show/Hide control at the left edge of the SmartArt graphic (**Figure 6.11**). Or you can choose SmartArt Tools > Create Graphic > Text Pane. Both these controls toggle the text pane's appearance and disappearance.

Figure 6.11 This control toggles the text pane on and off.

Formatting SmartArt

When a SmartArt graphic is selected on your slide, a new set of contextual tabs, the SmartArt Tools, appears on the Ribbon. These consist of two subtabs, Design and Format. On the Design tab, you can change the number of shapes in the graphic, switch to a different SmartArt layout, recolor the graphic, or apply some preset styles to give your SmartArt a whole new look (**Figure 6.12**). The Format tab allows you to modify the shapes in your graphic, apply styles to the individual shapes, apply WordArt and other text styling to the text in the SmartArt, and offers tools to set the alignment and size of the graphic (**Figure 6.13**).

In this section, we'll focus on changing the look of a SmartArt graphic. In the next section, we'll get into changing the structure and layout of SmartArt.

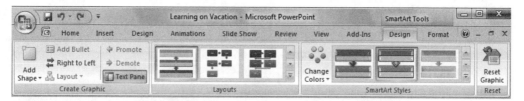

Figure 6.12 The Design subtab of SmartArt Tools.

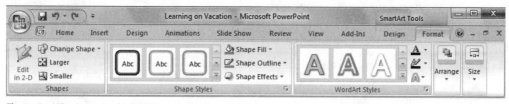

Figure 6.13 The Format subtab of SmartArt Tools.

To change the color of a SmartArt graphic:

1. Select the SmartArt you want to recolor.

2. Choose SmartArt Tools > Design > SmartArt Styles > Change Colors.

   The colors gallery appears (**Figure 6.14**). These color variations range from subtle to colorful. The gallery is likely to look different from the one shown here, because you'll probably have used another SmartArt layout.

3. Roll your mouse cursor over a color variation in the gallery. As you roll over a variation, PowerPoint shows you a live preview of what the color will look like.

4. Click your mouse on a color variation to select it and apply it to the SmartArt.

   The SmartArt graphic changes.

To apply a SmartArt Style:

1. Select the SmartArt you want to restyle.

2. Choose SmartArt Tools > Design > SmartArt Styles, then choose a style from the gallery.

   You can scroll through the gallery, or you can click the More button at the lower-right corner of the gallery to expand it and see all the styles (**Figure 6.15**). As usual, as you roll over a style in the gallery, PowerPoint shows you a live preview of what the style will look like. The gallery will probably look different from the one shown here, because your SmartArt will be different.

3. Click a style in the gallery to select it and apply it to the SmartArt.

   The SmartArt graphic changes.

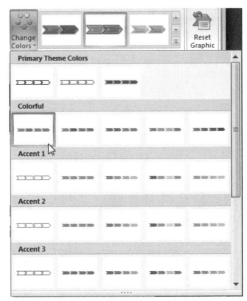

Figure 6.14 This gallery allows you to pick color variations for your SmartArt.

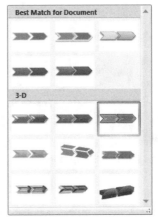

Figure 6.15
The style variations gallery include both 2-D and 3-D styles.

✔ Tip

■ If after further thought you don't like the changes that you made to the SmartArt graphic, choose SmartArt Tools > Design > Reset > Reset Graphic. All of the formatting changes you made to the graphic will be stripped away, leaving the graphic as though you had just inserted it. It also resizes the graphic to its original dimensions.

FORMATTING SMARTART

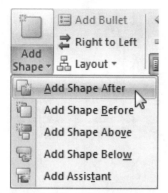

Figure 6.16 You will use this menu to add a shape to an existing SmartArt graphic.

Modifying SmartArt

Making changes to your SmartArt can mean any of a number of things. You might want to add a shape (or subtract one) from the shapes that appear when you insert the SmartArt. You might decide that a different layout would suit your diagram better. Some SmartArt layouts, the ones that show process in a horizontal direction, might benefit from reversing that direction. Or you might want to make your diagram bigger or smaller.

To add a shape to SmartArt:

1. Insert a SmartArt graphic on your slide.

   or

   Select an existing SmartArt graphic.

2. Click the existing shape that is closest to where you want the new shape to appear.

3. Choose SmartArt Tools > Design > Create Graphic, then click the arrow under Add Shape.

   The Add Shape menu appears (**Figure 6.16**).

continues on next page

4. Choose one of the following:

▲ Click **Add Shape After** to insert a shape at the same level as the selected shape, but following it.

▲ Click **Add Shape Before** to insert a shape at the same level as the selected shape, but before it.

▲ Click **Add Shape Above** to insert a shape one level above the selected shape.

▲ Click **Add Shape Below** to insert a shape one level below the selected shape.

▲ Click **Add Assistant** (only available if you are editing an organization chart) to add a shape one level below and connected to the selected shape.

The shape is added to your SmartArt graphic (**Figure 6.17**).

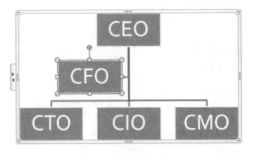

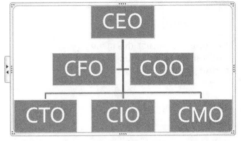

Figure 6.17 I used the Add Shape After menu choice to add another box on the same level as the CFO (bottom).

✔ Tips

■ Some SmartArt layouts can contain only a limited number of shapes, and if you exceed the maximum number of shapes, the message "Anything above marked with a red X will not appear in this SmartArt graphic and will not be saved" appears at the bottom of the text pane in your SmartArt graphic. If you switch to a different layout that isn't limited to a maximum number of shapes, the information below the red X will reappear in the SmartArt graphic.

■ To subtract a shape from SmartArt, simply select the shape and press Backspace.

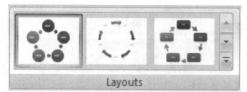

Figure 6.18 Choose your new SmartArt layout from the gallery.

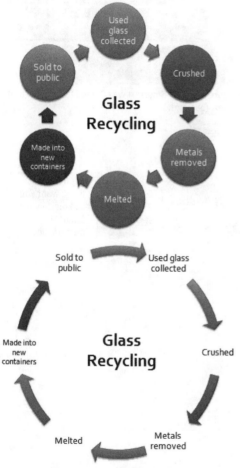

Figure 6.19 This recycling diagram was changed from circles and arrows (top) to just text and arrows (bottom).

To switch to a different SmartArt layout:

1. Select the SmartArt you want to change.

2. Choose SmartArt Tools > Design > Layouts, then choose a new layout from the gallery (**Figure 6.18**).

   The SmartArt layout changes (**Figure 6.19**).

✔ Tip

- If you have a layout with one of the embedded picture placeholders, and you have inserted pictures into the placeholders, the pictures will be lost when you switch to a different layout, and you will have to reinsert them if the new layout also has picture placeholders.

To flip a SmartArt graphic:

1. Select the SmartArt you want to change.

2. Click SmartArt Tools > Design > Create Graphic > Right to Left.

   The SmartArt flips as you command (**Figure 6.20**). This button acts as a toggle, so you can switch back just by clicking on it again. PowerPoint keeps the text readable, even though the shapes have flipped orientation.

To resize SmartArt:

1. Select the SmartArt you want to change.

2. Click and drag any of the edges or corners of the graphic.

   or

   Choose SmartArt Tools > Format > Size, then enter figures in the Height and Width fields (**Figure 6.21**).

   The SmartArt resizes to your specifications.

Figure 6.20 The SmartArt was flipped from right (top) to left (bottom).

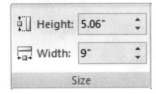

Figure 6.21 If you want you can resize your SmartArt numerically.

Figure 6.22 Use the shortcut menu to save the SmartArt as a picture.

Figure 6.23 Navigate to where you want the exported picture to go, give the new picture a name, and choose the file type.

Exporting a SmartArt Graphic

As you've seen earlier in this chapter, SmartArt can look pretty great. So great, in fact, that you might want to reuse SmartArt in another program, such as a page layout program or a Web page editor. One way to do that is to create the SmartArt graphic in PowerPoint (or in Word, Excel, or Outlook), then copy and paste it into the other program. But you can also export the SmartArt as a stand-alone graphics file, in the standard PNG, JPG, TIF, GIF or Windows Metafile formats.

To export a SmartArt as a picture:

1. Select the SmartArt graphic you want to export.

2. Right-click on the graphic, then choose Save as Picture from the shortcut menu (**Figure 6.22**).

   The Save As Picture dialog appears (**Figure 6.23**).

3. Navigate to where you want to save the file, then type a name in the File name field.

4. Choose the graphic format you want for the exported file from the Save as type pop-up menu.

   I recommend that you use PNG format. See the "Picking a Format" sidebar.

5. Click Save to save the file.

EXPORTING A SMARTART GRAPHIC

Picking a Format

The PNG and TIF formats are generally the best ones to use for export, because they maintain the quality of the SmartArt the best, with an edge going to the PNG format. PNG is also a cross-platform format, well-supported by virtually all other programs that handle graphics.

The exported PNG or TIF file has a transparent background, whereas the other formats do not. The PNG file is usually considerably smaller in terms of disk space than the TIF, and PNG is a Web-usable format, unlike TIF. The JPG format is "lossy," meaning that some pixels are thrown away to reduce file size, which could make some details fuzzier. Finally, exported GIF files have the major limitation of that format, namely only 256 colors, resulting in dithering and a poor look.

ADDING RICH MEDIA AND HYPERLINKS

7

Rich media is the omnibus term for sounds, music, animations, and video files that you can add to your slides to enhance your presentation. You might want to include an animation on a slide to show a dynamic process, or insert a video clip to illustrate one of your points.

Background music, sound effects, and narration can add interest to your presentation, especially if you plan to export the presentation as a movie for use on the Web. Sounds and music are less useful when you're giving the presentation live, because people generally want to hear you, not a fancy production.

You're familiar with hyperlinks from browsing the Web. In PowerPoint, you can add a hyperlink to either text or graphics, and the link can go to another slide in the presentation, to a Web page, and more.

In this chapter, you'll learn how to add music and sounds to slides; use movies in your presentation; and add hyperlinks.

Adding Sounds or Music

With PowerPoint, you can easily add sounds or music to any slide or to an entire presentation. This allows you to lay down a soundtrack for the presentation. But be wary of adding sounds, because usually there's no quicker way to annoy your audience than by adding superfluous sounds to your slides. However, there are certainly valid reasons for using sound in your presentations. For example, a presentation about music might use brief clips, or anthropologists could include snippets of a language they are studying.

To use a sound, you'll need the sound files to be on your hard disk in a format that your computer can play; those formats are listed in **Table 7.1**.

On most people's systems, the most convenient repository of music will be their music library, which will often be in Apple's iTunes.

To add sound or music to a slide:

1. Go to the slide where you want to add music.

2. Choose Insert > Media Clips > Sound. The Insert Sound dialog appears (**Figure 7.1**).

Table 7.1

Supported Audio File Formats		
FORMAT	EXTENSION	COMMENTS
AIFF	.aiff or .aif	Widely used format originated by Apple for use on the Mac. Uncompressed audio, so large file size.
AU	.au	UNIX audio file format.
MIDI	.midi or .mid	Musical Instruments Digital Interface. Standard interchange format for musical instruments and synthesizers.
MP3	.mp3	Popular compressed music and sound format; used by iTunes and most other jukebox software.
WAV	.wav	Windows audio format, with variable compression. File sizes can be large.
WMA	.wma	Windows Media Audio file. Compressed audio, so small file sizes.

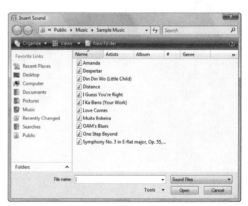

Figure 7.1 Choose the sound you want to add to your PowerPoint slide.

Figure 7.2 PowerPoint wants to know if the sound will play automatically or if you will trigger it manually.

Sound icon

• Bengal tiger - recorded 9/03

Figure 7.3 The music file appears on the slide as a small speaker icon.

Figure 7.4 The Sound Options group on the Sound Tools tab offers you several options to tweak sound playback.

3. Navigate to the sound you want, select it, and click Open.

PowerPoint asks if you want the sound to start automatically when you switch to the slide, or if it plays only when you click a button on the slide (**Figure 7.2**).

4. Click the button for the sound behavior you want.

An icon for the sound appears on the slide (**Figure 7.3**). The Sound Tools tab also appears in the Ribbon, containing two groups with sound settings (**Figure 7.4**).

5. (Optional) If you want to preview the sound, double-click the sound icon on the slide, or choose Sound Tools > Options > Play > Preview.

6. (Optional) In Sound Tools > Sound Options, pick one or more of the choices:

▲ **Hide During Show** hides the sound icon; otherwise, the icon will appear when you are giving the presentation.

▲ **Loop Until Stopped** repeats the sound until you click the slide or move to the next slide.

▲ **Play Sound** is a pop-up menu with three choices: Automatically, When Clicked, or Play Across Slides. The first option triggers the sound as soon as you move to the slide. The second option requires that you click on the sound icon during the show for the sound to play. And the third option starts the sound, and continues playing it for the length of the sound, even if you move to subsequent slides.

continues on next page

▲ **Max Sound File Size** governs the maximum size audio file PowerPoint will embed in the presentation file. Files larger than this will be linked to the PowerPoint presentation file. If you copy the file to another location, you must also copy the linked files to the same folder for the presentation to play correctly.

▲ **Slide Show Volume** lets you choose between Low, Medium, High, or Mute volume for the sound.

✔ Tips

■ The Play Across Slides option in the Play Sound pop-up menu doesn't allow you to specify the length of the sound; it just plays the whole sound regardless of what else is happening on screen. For better control, use the procedure under "To play a sound for a specified number of slides."

■ You can also hide sound icons by moving them off the slide into the area that surrounds the slide in Normal View. Of course, you can't click the sound icon during the show in that case, so you should set the sound to play automatically.

To play a sound for a specified number of slides:

1. Insert a sound as discussed in the previous procedure.

2. Click the sound icon on the slide to select it.

3. Choose Animations > Animations > Custom Animation (**Figure 7.5**).

   The Custom Animation task pane opens, with the sound file selected (**Figure 7.6**).

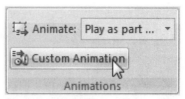

Figure 7.5 To set a sound to play for a specified number of slides, you must create a Custom Animation.

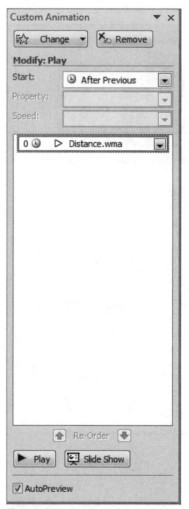

Figure 7.6 The Custom Animation task pane shows the sound file.

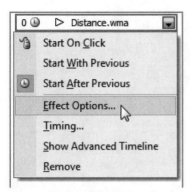

Figure 7.7 The pop-up menu next to the sound in the Custom Animation task pane allows you to set options.

Figure 7.8 Set the duration of the sound in the Stop playing section.

4. Click the arrow to the right of the sound file, and from the pop-up menu, choose Effect Options (**Figure 7.7**).

The Play Sound dialog appears (**Figure 7.8**).

5. In the Stop playing section, click the After radio button, then choose the number of slides you want in the box next to the button.

6. Click OK to dismiss the Play Sound dialog.

7. Click the close button in the Custom Animation task pane to close it.

✔ Tip

■ The most popular audio formats are MP3 and WMA. If you're going to be sharing your presentation with colleagues who will want to open it up with PowerPoint on the Mac, I recommend you avoid the use of WMA files and use MP3 or AIFF files instead. That's because there are many different kinds of WMA files, and not all of them will play on the Mac, since Microsoft no longer makes Windows Media Player available for the Mac.

ADDING SOUNDS OR MUSIC

127

Adding Slide Narration

You can add slide narration to any individual slide, or you can create one narration track that plays throughout the entire slideshow. I recommend individual files for presentations where the user will be controlling the advance of the slides.

You can add a narration file that you record with other software to the slide, or you can record sound into PowerPoint. Recording isn't especially difficult, but it does take some preparation. You'll need a number of pieces of hardware and software to record narration, including:

- A PC running Windows

- A microphone, sound card, and speakers

- Audio recording software (if you don't want to record directly into PowerPoint)

Windows has the ability to accept sound input from a variety of audio devices. Some PCs, such as notebooks, have microphones built-in, although these are not very good quality and you will probably not want to use them for narration, except in a pinch. If your PC has a line in or microphone port, you can plug a microphone into it. Some PCs do not have line in ports, and you will have to purchase a USB headset that contains headphones and a microphone (I like those by Plantronics (www.plantronics.com), but there are many other manufacturers), or purchase a USB audio adapter, such as Griffin Technology's iMic (www.griffintechnology.com). Despite the name, the iMic works on either Windows or Mac.

Microphones vary in price and quality. There are a wide variety of headset microphones that will serve nicely for recording narration, at prices well under $100.

Figure 7.9 To record narration, begin on the Slide Show tab.

Figure 7.10 Most of the time you'll need to increase the quality setting when recording narration files.

For many purposes, recording narration into PowerPoint will work just fine. But there are circumstances where you might need more control. For example, if your presentation will appear on the Web or be played without you present, you might want to record narration to a separate sound program, then use that program to edit the file, perhaps cutting out any mistakes or audio blemishes. You could even use a sound editing program to mix music or sound effects into your narration track. There are many audio editing and recording programs available; perhaps the best known is the free, open-source Audacity (`audacity.sourceforge.net`).

✔ Tips

- When you're searching for audio hardware or software, look at the products that are recommended for recording podcasts. They are just as appropriate for recording narration.

- Another possibility for audio recording and editing, if you have access to a Mac, is to use Apple's GarageBand software.

To record narration into PowerPoint:

1. Plug your microphone into your PC.

2. Launch PowerPoint.

   It's better to have the microphone available before you start PowerPoint; sometimes the mic won't be recognized if you attach it while PowerPoint is already running.

3. Open the presentation.

4. In the Normal View Pane, click to select the slide where you want to start the narration.

5. Choose Slide Show > Set Up > Record Narration (**Figure 7.9**).

   The Record Narration dialog appears (**Figure 7.10**).

continues on next page

ADDING SLIDE NARRATION

6. (Optional, but recommended) To adjust the recording quality and file size, click Change Quality.

The Sound Selection dialog appears (**Figure 7.11**).

By default, PowerPoint records at a low quality setting, which has the benefit of small file size. I prefer the setting Radio Quality, which has a decent compromise between file size and higher quality.

If you agree, choose Radio Quality from the Name pop-up menu, then click OK to return to the Record Narration dialog.

7. In the Record Narration dialog, click OK.

If you started recording on the first slide, PowerPoint begins Slide Show mode and the recording begins. Speak your narration.

or

If you were not on the first slide, PowerPoint asks if you want to start on the first slide or the current slide. Make your choice. PowerPoint begins Slide Show mode and starts recording. Speak your narration.

8. Click the slide to advance the presentation, as usual.

9. At the end of the presentation, PowerPoint shows the black Exit screen. Click anywhere on the screen to halt the recording and exit Slide Show mode.

While you were recording, PowerPoint also recorded slide timings, which tells you the amount of time spent on each slide, and the total presentation time.

10. PowerPoint presents a dialog asking if you want to keep the slide timings.

If you click Save, PowerPoint drops into Slide Sorter mode, where you can review the timing for each slide. If you click Don't Save, you're returned to Normal View.

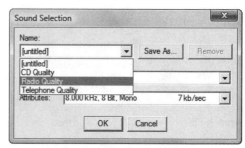

Figure 7.11 The Radio Quality setting is a nice balance between quality and file size.

✔ Tip

■ You can use this narration recording procedure either before the presentation, or during it, allowing you to record the audience's comments, too.

Figure 7.12 To bring sound into your presentation, use the pop-up menu under the Sound button.

To add separate narration files to your presentation:

1. In PowerPoint, go to the slide where you want to add narration.

2. Choose Insert > Media Clips > Sound, then click the arrow below the Sound button to bring up the pop-up menu and choose Sound from File (**Figure 7.12**). The Insert Sound dialog appears.

3. Navigate to the narration file you want, then choose Open.

   A sound icon appears on the slide.

To play a narration file:

◆ Double-click the sound icon on the slide.

✔ Tip

■ When you are recording audio narration, speak and enunciate clearly, using a measured pace. On the other hand, don't use a plodding pace. You want to shoot for a pace that is slightly slower than normal conversation, but that isn't inter-preted as you speaking deliberately slowly. Think back to the narration that you've heard in TV programs, and try to use that sort of pace.

Inserting Movies

Adding video files to your presentation can be a powerful tool that enhances your talk. Or it can be a needless bit of fluff that doesn't really help your presentation. Which is to say that you should give some serious thought before you put video in your slideshow.

Video clips must be on your computer in a format that PowerPoint can accept, as shown in **Table 7.2**.

To add movies to your presentation:

1. In PowerPoint, go to the slide where you want to add a movie.

2. If the slide contains a content box, click the Media icon (**Figure 7.13**).

   or

   If the slide doesn't have a content box, choose Insert > Media Clips > Movie.
   The Insert Media dialog appears.

3. Navigate to the movie file you want, then click Open.

   The movie appears on the slide, and PowerPoint asks if you want the movie to play automatically or only when clicked (**Figure 7.14**).

4. Make your choice of playback options.

5. If needed, drag the movie to position it where you want it on the slide.

Table 7.2

Supported Video File Formats		
FORMAT	EXTENSION	COMMENTS
WMF	.asf	Windows Media File in Advanced Streaming Format. Optimized for streaming media over a network.
Windows Video	.avi	Most popular Windows video format; wide range of compression schemes.
Movie	.mpg or .mpeg	Standard video format, widely used on UNIX machines.
Windows Media Video	.wmv	Windows Media Video; another popular Microsoft-developed video format.

Figure 7.13 Click the film reel icon in the content box to insert a movie file.

Figure 7.14 PowerPoint will play the movie automatically or at your command.

INSERTING MOVIES

Figure 7.15 Use Movie Options to adjust movie playback.

Previewing and controlling movies

When you select a movie on a slide, the Movie Tool tab appears in the Ribbon, allowing you to set some of the movie's playback options.

To preview a movie:

◆ Double-click the movie on the slide.

or

◆ With the movie selected, choose Movie Tools > Play > Preview (**Figure 7.15**).

To set a movie's playback properties:

1. Select the movie.

2. In Movie Tools > Movie Options, set one or more of the options:

   ▲ **Play Movie** is a pop-up menu with three choices: Automatically, When Clicked, or Play Across Slides. The first option triggers the movie as soon as you move to the slide. The second option requires that you click on the movie during the show for the video to play. And the third option starts the movie, and continues playing it for the length of the video, even if you move to subsequent slides.

   ▲ **Hide During Show** hides the movie; otherwise, the video will appear when you are giving the presentation. This option seems to be buggy and not work; I recommend you avoid it.

   ▲ **Play Full Screen** makes the movie take up the entire screen on playback, hiding the slide.

   ▲ **Loop Until Stopped** repeats the movie until you click the slide or move to the next slide.

continues on next page

Hey, Where's QuickTime?

Apple's QuickTime multimedia file format supports dozens of audio and video file formats. It is available for Mac and Windows, and is often used to stream video content from Web sites. QuickTime is also very popular, because anyone who owns an iPod needs to use iTunes, which requires QuickTime.

PowerPoint used to support QuickTime movies on slides, but that ability was removed in PowerPoint 2007. I know of no good way to get a QuickTime movie running inside PowerPoint. Instead, you have two workarounds:

◆ **Convert** the QuickTime movie into one of the supported video formats, usually WMV or AVI. You can convert to AVI using Apple's $30 QuickTime Pro. For WMV conversion, take a look at Flip4Mac WMV Studio ($50; www.flip4mac.com).

◆ **Hyperlink** to the QuickTime movie from one of your slides. Clicking the link will launch the QuickTime for Windows player, and play the movie. Then you can return to your presentation.

- ▲ **Rewind Movie After Playing** makes the video play once, then return to the first frame.

- ▲ **Slide Show Volume** lets you choose between Low, Medium, High, or Mute volume for the sound.

✔ Tips

- Movie files can be resized. Just click the movie on the slide to select it, and drag the resize handles that appear. Be aware that if you scale the movie up more than a little bit, the video quality will degrade.

- Slower machines sometimes have problems playing full-screen movies within PowerPoint (that is, movies that take up the entire area of the slide). Video tends to stutter and not run smoothly. You should, as always, be sure to play your presentation through before you give your talk.

- If you double-click a movie on the slide, it will start playing; click it again to pause it.

- You can add more than one movie to a slide.

- Media files tend to be big. A movie can easily take up tens or even hundreds of megabytes of disk space. By default, PowerPoint doesn't save media files, such as sounds or movies, in the presentation file. Instead, it stores links to the media files. If you copy your presentation file to another computer without also copying the external media files, the media files will be lost to the presentation. To avoid this, make sure that you keep the external media files in the same folder as the presentation file.

INSERTING MOVIES

Adding Flash Animations

Adobe Flash movies are the most popular animation format, used for most animations you see on the Web. Flash is great for creating animated logos, animations that describe a process, or even cool animated charts for use in your presentations. Because Flash animations are usually vector graphics, you can scale the Flash movie on your slide with no loss of quality.

Unfortunately, while PowerPoint has the ability to play some Flash files, Microsoft hasn't made it easy to do so. Playing a Flash movie requires a complicated process that includes enabling hidden options in PowerPoint, installing an ActiveX control on each slide that contains Flash, then setting several properties for each animation you want to use. To discover this Byzantine process, search for "Play an Adobe Macromedia Flash animation in a presentation" in PowerPoint Help.

Figure 7.16 Begin creating a hyperlink in the Insert Hyperlink dialog.

Adding Hyperlinks

You're already familiar with the concept of hyperlinks from using a Web browser. In PowerPoint, you can use a hyperlink to connect either text or a graphic to another PowerPoint slide, a Web page, another PowerPoint presentation, or to create an email message. You can also use a hyperlink to exit the presentation.

When you click a link that opens a Web page during your presentation, your PC leaves PowerPoint, switches to your default Web browser, brings it to the front, and loads the page specified by the link in a window. When you are done with the browser and wish to return to the presentation, simply click on the visible portion of the slide behind the browser window. You'll go right back into your presentation, picking up where you left off.

To link to a Web page:

You can create a text link on a slide by typing the link's URL, and PowerPoint will automatically make the link clickable. But if you want to make regular text on the slide or a graphic into a link, follow these steps:

1. Select the object you want to use as the hyperlink.

   This can be either text or a graphic.

2. Choose Insert > Links > Hyperlink, or press Ctrl K.

   The Insert Hyperlink dialog appears (**Figure 7.16**).

continues on next page

3. In the Address field, type the full Web address for the hyperlink. If the address starts with www., PowerPoint will automatically add the http:// before the address. If it does not, as in office.microsoft.com, you must add the http:// manually.

If you selected text, the text becomes underlined (**Figure 7.17**). Graphic objects appear the same as before.

4. Click OK.

When you run the presentation, clicking a link on the slide brings up your default Web browser (**Figure 7.18**).

✔ Tip

■ Any text you type on a slide that begins with "www", "ftp", or "http" will automatically become a hyperlink.

Figure 7.17 You can turn specific text into a link, and URLs that you type onto the slide will automatically become links.

Figure 7.18 When you leave the presentation to view a Web page, your browser appears in front of the slide. Just click the slide to return to your show.

Figure 7.19 Use the Place in This Document choice to jump to a different slide in the presentation.

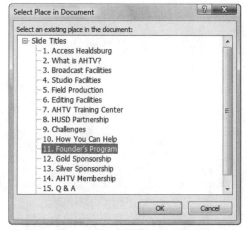

Figure 7.20 When you're linking to a different PowerPoint presentation, you need to specify where in the document you want to go.

To link to another slide in the same presentation:

1. Select the object you want to use as the hyperlink.

   This can be either text or a graphic.

2. Choose Insert > Links > Hyperlink, or press Ctrl K.

   The Insert Hyperlink dialog appears.

3. In the Link to section of the Insert Hyperlink dialog, click Place in This Document.

   The dialog changes to reflect your choice (**Figure 7.19**).

4. In the scrolling list, choose the slide that you want to jump to.

   A preview appears on the right side of the dialog.

5. Click OK.

✔ Tip

■ There are other choices under Place in This Document, including First Slide, Last Slide, Next Slide, and Previous Slide. These give you additional navigation choices.

To link to a slide in another PowerPoint presentation:

1. Select the text or graphic you want to use as the hyperlink.

2. Choose Insert > Links > Hyperlink, or press Ctrl K.

   The Insert Hyperlink dialog appears.

3. In the Link to column, click Existing File or Web Page.

4. Navigate to and click to select the PowerPoint file you want to link to.

5. Click Bookmark.

   The Select Place in Document dialog appears (**Figure 7.20**).

6. Click to select the slide you want to link to, then click OK.

ADDING HYPERLINKS

To link to a new email message:

1. Select the text or graphic you want to use as the hyperlink.

2. Choose Insert > Links > Hyperlink, or press ⌃Ctrl⌃K.

   The Insert Hyperlink dialog appears.

3. In the Link to column, click E-mail address.

   The dialog changes to reflect your choice (**Figure 7.21**).

4. Enter the destination email address in the E-mail address field and the email's subject line in the Subject field.

5. Click OK.

Figure 7.21 Address the email message that will be created when the link is clicked.

✔ Tips

■ You probably wouldn't be using email hyperlinks in a presentation you are projecting for an audience, because it's hard to imagine you would want to compose an email in the middle of your show. Email links are more likely to be used in a self-running presentation.

■ The new email will be created in your default email program.

Secret Links

You can use buttons and links to change the order of your presentation on the fly, without your audience even noticing.

For example, let's say that you're giving a sales presentation, and you come to a slide introducing a new product line. If the audience is receptive, simply continue on to the next slide. But what if you get a negative reaction? Some creative linking can give you a Plan B. Create a graphic object that matches the slide background or has a transparency setting of 100% (so it's invisible to the audience) and apply a hyperlink that jumps to a particular slide. This emergency exit button will let you skip to the next section without ever appearing to lose your cool.

This trick can also come in handy for those of us who sometimes run out of time before finishing all of our slides. Put an invisible button on all your slides that jumps right to the closing one.

WORKING WITH TABLES

In presentations, you'll often find it useful to present data in tables. A table's rows and columns make it easy to present complex information in a simple way. Examples of such data would be quarterly financial results, a performance comparison of two or more products, or even a simple list.

PowerPoint provides an excellent set of tools for creating and formatting tables and their contents. These tools allow you to make even dry financial data visually interesting. Using object builds, you can also make parts of your table animate onto the screen, allowing you to build your points one step at a time. You'll find more information about using animation in Chapter 10.

In this chapter, you'll learn how to use PowerPoint to create and modify a table, and ensure that tables and their content look the way you intend.

Creating a Table

Tables consist of rows and columns. *Rows* are the horizontal divisions of the table; *columns* are the vertical divisions. A row and a column intersect to form a *cell*, which is where the content of the table goes. You can put either text or a graphic (or both) into a cell.

When you add a table to a slide, PowerPoint allows you to create a table with whatever number of rows and columns you want. After the table is added, you can modify the table and its contents by changing the table's graphic design or the number of rows and columns, formatting the text, modifying table and cell borders, and changing the size of the table.

You're probably familiar with using tables in word processors, such as Microsoft Word. Using tables in PowerPoint is similar, with one important caveat: tables in presentations should be simpler than tables that you would use in a printed document. Too much information in a table can overwhelm the viewer (**Figure 8.1**).

To create a table:

1. In the Normal View pane, select the slide on which you wish to create a table, or create a new slide by choosing Home > Slides > New Slide.

2. If you created a new slide, choose an appropriate slide layout using the Layout pop-up menu in the Home > Slides group.

   Because you want to leave enough room on the slide for the table, you'll probably want to choose a slide master such as Blank, Title and Content, or Title Only. PowerPoint attempts to place tables so that they will fit properly on the slide, so, for example, if you choose the Two Content layout, adding a table will create a small table in one of the content boxes on the slide.

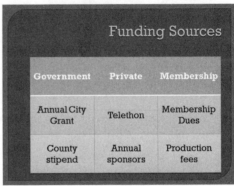

Figure 8.1 Too much information in a table will make the table too hard for your audience to read (top). It's best to keep tables for presentations simple (bottom).

CREATING A TABLE

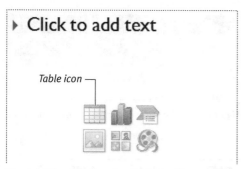

Table icon

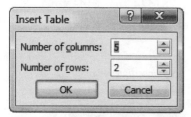

Figure 8.2 On slide layouts with content boxes, click the table icon to create your table.

Figure 8.3 Specify the number of rows and columns you want your table to have.

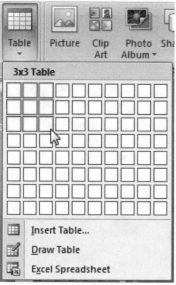

Figure 8.4 With the Table pop-up menu in the Ribbon, you can size your table by dragging.

3. If your layout has a content box, click its table icon (**Figure 8.2**).

The Insert Table dialog appears (**Figure 8.3**).

Choose the number of rows and columns for the table, then click OK. The table appears on your slide.

or

If your layout does not have a content box, choose Insert > Tables > Table.

The Table button is a pop-up menu that allows you to select the number of rows and columns by dragging (**Figure 8.4**). Drag to the table size you want, then release the mouse button.

The table appears on the slide (**Figure 8.5**). To increase the number of rows and/or columns, see "Inserting Rows and Columns," later in this chapter.

✔ Tip

■ When you're inserting a table into a content box, the table becomes the width of the box. On a layout without a content box, the table is about 60% of the slide width.

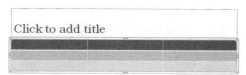

Click to add title

Figure 8.5 This table has a default style applied to it by the overall presentation design.

Selecting Table Elements

To work effectively with a table, you'll need to know how to select its elements. You can select an entire table; one or more rows and columns; an individual cell or multiple cells; and nonadjacent cells, rows, or columns.

To select the entire table:

◆ Click once anywhere in the table.

Eight selection handles appear at the edges of the table; use them to resize the table, as described later in the chapter (**Figure 8.6**).

To select a single cell and its contents:

◆ Move the mouse pointer near the left edge of a cell until the cursor changes to an arrow pointing to the upper right, then click (**Figure 8.7**).

To select just a cell's contents:

◆ Hold down the Control key, position the mouse pointer in the cell and to the left of its contents, and click.

To place a text insertion point in a cell:

◆ Click inside a cell. A text insertion point appears inside the cell (**Figure 8.8**).

When the insertion point appears in a table cell, you can move the cursor between table cells by pressing Tab.

To select a contiguous group of cells:

◆ Click in the first cell, and drag to the last cell you want to select.

or

Click the first cell, hold down the Shift key, then click the last cell.

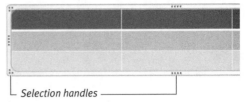
Selection handles
Figure 8.6 Use the selection handles to resize the table.

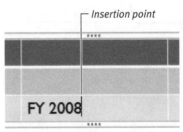

$162	$141	$148
$120	$117	$116
$152	$149	$144

Figure 8.7 The highlighted cell is selected.

Insertion point
FY 2008
Figure 8.8 When you click in a cell, the text insertion point appears.

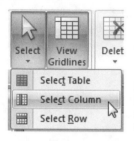

Division	Q1	Q2	Q3	Q4	Goal %
North	$162	$141	$148	$152	-5%
East	$120	$117	$116	$121	-7%
West	$152	$149	$144	$146	-2%

Figure 8.9 The highlighted row (highlighted in blue, though you can't see that in this black-and-white picture) is selected.

Select | View Gridlines | Delet

☐ Select Table
☐ Select Column
☐ Select Row

Figure 8.10 Use the Select pop-up menu to select the whole table, a row, or a column.

Figure 8.11 The cursor changes depending on whether you are moving (left) or copying (right) cell contents.

The selected cells will be highlighted in blue (**Figure 8.9**). You can use these techniques to select any rectangular group of cells, be it a row, column, or any other area of the table.

You can also use the Table Tools > Layout > Table > Select to select a row or a column (**Figure 8.10**). Click in a cell, then make a choice from the pop-up menu under the Select button. You can also use this to select the entire table.

To move or copy the contents of one cell into another:

1. To move a cell's contents, select the contents of a single cell, hold down the mouse button for a moment, then drag the contents to another cell.

   or

   To copy the cell's contents, select the contents of a single cell, hold down the mouse button for a moment, press the Control key, then drag the contents to another cell.

   As you drag, you'll see the cursor change. The cursor looks different, depending on whether you are moving or copying cell contents (**Figure 8.11**).

2. When you reach the destination cell, release the mouse button.

   The contents of the first cell will be moved or copied into the second cell.

✔ Tips

- The cell contents you are dragging will be appended to the contents of the destination cell, if any.

- If you select multiple cells (like a row or a column) and drag, the contents of all the cells will be *moved* to the destination cells. If you select multiple cells and Control-drag, the contents of all the cells will be *copied* into the destination cells.

Resizing Table Elements

You can resize tables horizontally or vertically, and also make columns wider and rows taller.

To resize an entire table:

1. Click anywhere in a table to select it. The selection handles will appear at the edges of the table (see Figure 8.6).

2. Drag one of the selection handles. To widen the table, drag the handle on the right edge of the table; to make the table taller, drag the handle on the bottom edge of the table; and to make the table grow in both directions simultaneously, drag the handle at the bottom-right corner of the table.

✔ Tip

- If you hold down the Shift key when resizing the table, it will resize the horizontal and vertical axes proportionately.

To resize a row or column:

1. Click once outside the table to make sure that no table element is selected, then click once in the table to select it.

2. As you hover your cursor over a border between two rows or two columns, it will turn into a double-headed arrow (**Figure 8.12**).

3. Drag the border to resize the row or column.

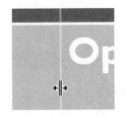

Figure 8.12 When the cursor turns into a double-headed arrow, you can drag it to move a row or column border.

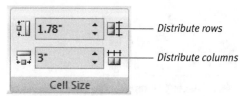

Figure 8.13 Use the buttons in the Cell Size group to make rows and columns evenly spaced.

QI	Q2	Q3	Q4	Goal %
$162	$141	$148	$152	-5%
$120	$117	$116	$121	-7%
$152	$149	$144	$146	-2%
$110	$112	$111	$113	+1%
$14	$14	$15	$15	+12%
$9	$11	$14	$13	+10%
$1	$2	$1.5	$2	n/a
$91	$94	$93	$92	+2%
$26	$28	$30	$34	+11%

QI	Q2	Q3	Q4	Goal %
$162	$141	$148	$152	-5%
$120	$117	$116	$121	-7%
$152	$149	$144	$146	-2%
$110	$112	$111	$113	+1%
$14	$14	$15	$15	+12%
$9	$11	$14	$13	+10%
$1	$2	$1.5	$2	n/a
$91	$94	$93	$92	+2%
$26	$28	$30	$34	+11%

Figure 8.14 I've made all of the columns the same width with the Distribute columns button.

To distribute row heights or column widths evenly:

1. Select a table that has some rows taller than others, or some columns wider than others.

2. Depending on what you want to do, choose Table Tools > Layout > Cell Size > Distribute Rows, or choose Table Tools > Layout > Cell Size > Distribute Columns (**Figure 8.13**).

   PowerPoint will even out the space between rows or columns, depending on what you chose (**Figure 8.14**).

Deleting Table Elements

PowerPoint makes it easy to remove tables, cell contents, rows, or columns.

To delete a table:

1. Click the table's border to select it.

2. Press Backspace.

To delete the contents of cells:

1. Select one or more cells.

2. Press Backspace.

To delete rows:

1. Select one or more rows.

2. Press Backspace.

   or

   Choose Table Tools > Layout > Rows & Columns > Delete, then choose Delete Rows from the pop-up menu (**Figure 8.15**).

To delete columns:

1. Select one or more columns.

2. Press Backspace.

   or

   Choose Table Tools > Layout > Rows & Columns > Delete, then choose Delete Columns from the pop-up menu.

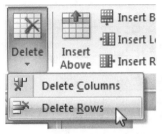

Figure 8.15 You can use the Ribbon to delete table elements.

Inserting Rows and Columns

PowerPoint allows you to add rows or columns to your table, either by adding rows or columns to the overall table, or by inserting rows or columns at a selected spot in the table.

PowerPoint usually includes a *header row* at the top of your table. A header row is formatted differently than the rest of the table to highlight the information in the headers (the exact formatting is specified by the table design). You would typically use the contents of a header row as labels for information in the rest of the table.

You can also have PowerPoint automatically apply different formatting for three other parts of the table:

◆ The *total row* is the bottom row of the table.

◆ The *first column* is the leftmost column in the table.

◆ The *last column* is the rightmost column in the table.

To specially style one row or column:

1. Click the table's border to select it.

   The Table Tools contextual tab appears, with two subtabs: Design and Layout.

2. In the Table Tools > Design > Table Style Options group, choose one or more of the following (**Figure 8.16**):

   ▲ Header Row

   ▲ Total Row

   ▲ First Column

   ▲ Last Column

   ▲ Banded Rows makes the background color of alternating rows lighter and darker, to improve readability.

   ▲ Banded Columns makes the background color of alternating columns lighter and darker, to improve readability.

   PowerPoint styles the rows or columns you chose.

✔ Tip

- Sometimes the table design overrides the settings in the Table Style Options group. Choose a different table design, if needed. See "Applying Table Designs," later in this chapter.

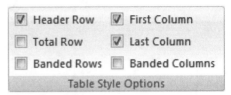

Figure 8.16 A header row and first column are formatted differently than the rest of the table, so they stand out.

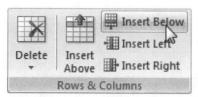

Figure 8.17 You can use the Ribbon to insert rows and columns...

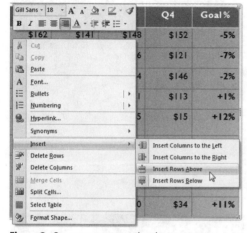

Figure 8.18 ...or you can use the shortcut menu.

To insert rows in a table:

1. Click anywhere in a row.

2. Choose Table Tools > Layout > Rows & Columns, then click either Insert Above or Insert Below (**Figure 8.17**).

   PowerPoint inserts an empty row above or below your selection, depending on which button you used. This will also increase the height of the table.

✔ Tip

- You can also right-click and choose Insert > Insert Rows Above or Insert > Insert Rows Below from the resulting shortcut menu (**Figure 8.18**).

To insert columns in a table:

1. Click anywhere in a column.

2. Choose Table Tools > Layout > Rows & Columns, then click either Insert Left or Insert Right.

   PowerPoint inserts an empty column before or after your selection, depending on which button you used. Unexpectedly, this does not increase the table's width.

✔ Tips

- As with rows, you can right-click and choose Insert > Insert Columns to the Left or Insert > Insert Column to the Right from the resulting shortcut menu (Figure 8.18).

- Though the shortcut menu choices refer to "Rows" and "Columns," those menu choices only add one row or column at a time.

Merging and Splitting Cells

PowerPoint lets you *merge cells*, which is combining two or more adjacent cells into one larger cell, or you can split a single cell into two or more cells, either vertically or horizontally.

Merge Cells
Split Cells
Merge

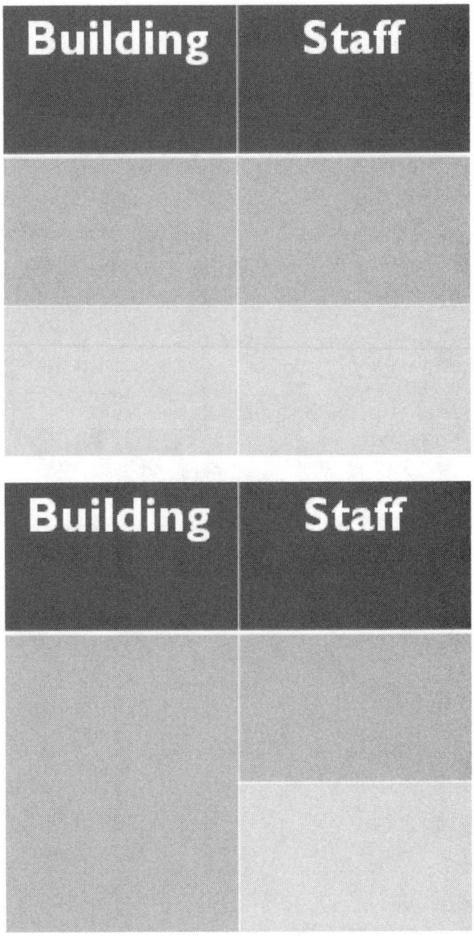

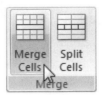

Figure 8.19 Click Merge Cells to eliminate the border between two cells.

To merge cells:

1. Select the cells you want to merge.
2. Choose Table Tools > Layout > Merge > Merge Cells (**Figure 8.19**).

   or

   Right-click the selection and choose Merge Cells from the contextual menu.

   The cells merge (**Figure 8.20**).

Building
Staff
Building
Staff

Figure 8.20 First there were two cells (top), then there was one (bottom).

✔ Tip

- You can merge an entire row or column into one cell. The contents, if any, of the row or column will be incorporated into the new cell, and if necessary, text will wrap to fit in the new cell.

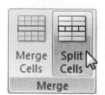

Figure 8.21 Click Split Cells to break a cell into two or more cells.

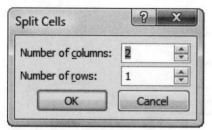

Figure 8.22 Specify the number of rows and columns for the split.

To split cells:

1. Select the cells you want to split.

2. Choose Table Tools > Layout > Merge > Split Cells (**Figure 8.21**).

   or

   Right-click the selection and choose Split Cells from the contextual menu.

   The Split Cells dialog appears (**Figure 8.22**).

3. Set the number of rows and columns you want the cell to split into, then click OK.

   The cell splits as you command.

✔ Tip

■ If you select more than one cell, PowerPoint will split all of them evenly.

MERGING AND SPLITTING CELLS

Working with Cell Borders

To dress up your tables, PowerPoint allows you to style and modify the borders between cells. You can change a border's color, line weight, or line style. If you would like to create or eliminate a border, PowerPoint also provides border drawing and erasing tools.

To style cell borders:

1. Click anywhere in a table to select it. The Table Tools contextual tab appears in the Ribbon.

2. In the Table Tools > Design > Draw Borders group (**Figure 8.23**), do one or more of the following:

   ▲ From the Pen Style pop-up menu, choose the kind of line you will draw (**Figure 8.24**).

   ▲ Select the thickness of the line from the Pen Weight pop-up menu (**Figure 8.25**).

   ▲ Set the color of the line from the Pen Color pop-up menu (**Figure 8.26**).

   After you've made your selection from the pop-up menus, the Draw Table button highlights and the cursor turns into a pencil.

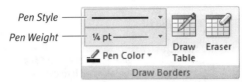

Figure 8.23 Use the Draw Border group's controls to set the line thickness, style, and color for borders.

Figure 8.24 The Pen Style pop-up menu gives you several line styles.

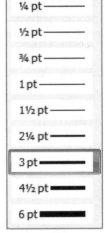

Figure 8.25 The Pen Weight pop-up menu lets you set the line thickness.

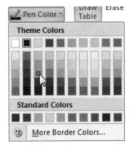

Figure 8.26 Pick a color from the Pen Color pop-up menu.

Figure 8.27 The result of a changed border.

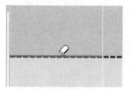

Figure 8.28 Begin drawing the line (left) to split the cell (right).

Figure 8.29 Click a border with the Eraser tool to eliminate it.

3. Use the pencil cursor to draw over one of the existing borders.

The border changes to match the settings you made in the Draw Borders group (**Figure 8.27**).

To draw cell borders:

1. You can also use the Draw Table button in the Draw Borders group to add additional borders (and therefore to split table cells). Begin by setting the pen style, weight, and color.

The Draw Table button highlights and the cursor turns into a pencil.

2. Draw a line within a cell to split it into two rows or two columns (**Figure 8.28**).

To erase cell borders:

1. If you want to subtract a border between two table cells, choose Table Tools > Design > Draw Borders > Eraser.

The Eraser button highlights and the cursor turns into an eraser.

2. Click the Eraser on the cell border you wish to eliminate.

The border disappears (**Figure 8.29**). Because you have eliminated a border between cells, the cells merge.

✔ Tip

■ With the Draw Table or Eraser tool, if it's highlighted and then you decide that you would rather turn off the tools and not make any changes, just click outside of the table to deselect the tool.

WORKING WITH CELL BORDERS

Applying Table Designs

Once you have the layout of your table set to your liking, you can turn your attention to the formatting of the text and graphics within the table. Much of the time, this will be done for you, because PowerPoint's table styles are part of the presentation's overall design theme. When you assign a theme (see Chapter 2 for more on themes), PowerPoint supplies a number of table styles that complement the rest of the theme's background, font, layout, and chart styles. You can, of course, override the program's design choices if they aren't to your liking. Like most other style choices in PowerPoint, when you apply a table style, you choose from a gallery, and PowerPoint displays a live preview of your choice.

To set a table's design:

1. Click anywhere in a table to select it.

   The Table Tools contextual tab appears in the Ribbon.

2. In the Design tab of Table Tools, hover your mouse cursor over the styles in the gallery within the Table Styles group (**Figure 8.30**).

   The table shows a live preview of the style thumbnail you are hovering over.

3. Click the style thumbnail to apply that style to the table.

   The table changes.

   or

   To see more styles, click the More button in the gallery.

   The gallery expands to show all the styles (**Figure 8.31**). Click a style thumbnail to apply that style to the table.

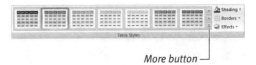

More button

Figure 8.30 Click one of the table styles in this gallery to apply that style.

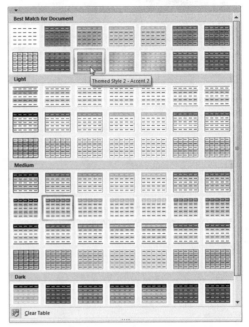

Figure 8.31 PowerPoint provides dozens of table styles that match your presentation design.

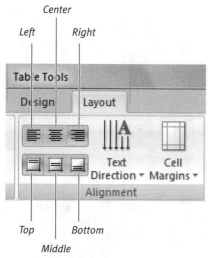

Center

Left   Right

Top   Bottom

Middle

Figure 8.32 Use the alignment controls in the Alignment group for both horizontal and vertical alignment of text.

Building	Staff	Equipment
Remaining tasks: •Studio floor to be refinished •Install light grid •Change locks •Purchase furniture	Hire: •Executive director •Operations manager •Production instructor •Playback technician	Arrived: •Video server •Equipment racks •Studio cameras •Video Toaster •BBS computer

Building	Staff	Equipment
Remaining tasks: •Studio floor to be refinished •Install light grid •Change locks •Purchase furniture	Hire: •Executive director •Operations manager •Production instructor •Playback technician	Arrived: •Video server •Equipment racks •Studio cameras •Video Toaster •BBS computer

Building	Staff	Equipment
Remaining tasks: •Studio floor to be refinished •Install light grid •Change locks •Purchase furniture	Hire: •Executive director •Operations manager •Production instructor •Playback technician	Arrived: •Video server •Equipment racks •Studio cameras •Video Toaster •BBS computer

Figure 8.33 Horizontal text alignment within table cells. From top to bottom: Left, Center, and Right text alignment.

Styling Cell Contents

You can set alignment for the contents of all of the cells, and there are separate controls for horizontal and vertical alignment, and also for text direction. The alignment controls work for text within the cell, but not graphics, which float in a separate layer from the table. Working with cell backgrounds, another table attribute, will be covered in "Adding Cell Backgrounds and Graphics," later in this chapter.

If you want to apply alignment to the contents of a single cell, or group of cells, you must select the cell or cells first. In addition to text alignment, you have the same control over the text in tables that you do with any text in PowerPoint. See Chapter 4 for more information about text handling in PowerPoint. You can also control how large the margins are within table cells.

To set alignment in cells:

1. Select the cells to which you wish to apply text alignment.

2. Use the alignment tools in the Table Tools > Layout > Alignment group to set your desired text alignment (**Figure 8.32**). You can set horizontal alignment (**Figure 8.33**) and vertical alignment (**Figure 8.34**) separately.

Building	Staff

Building	Staff

Building	Staff

Figure 8.34 Vertical text alignment within table cells. From left to right: Top, Center, and Bottom alignment.

To set text direction:

1. If you want to rotate text within a cell, you can set the *text direction*. Begin by selecting the cell or cells where you want to rotate the text.

2. Choose Table Tools > Layout > Alignment > Text Direction, then make a choice from the resulting pop-up menu.

   The preset choices are Horizontal, Rotate all text 90°, Rotate all text 270°, or Stacked (**Figure 8.35**).

   The text in the cells changes as you command.

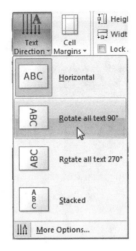

Figure 8.35 Change the orientation of text with the Text Direction pop-up menu.

To apply and change cell margins:

1. Select the table, or if you only wish to make changes to a particular set of cells, select those cells.

2. Choose Table Tools > Layout > Alignment > Cell Margins, then make a choice from the resulting pop-up menu.

   The preset choices are Normal, None, Narrow, or Wide (**Figure 8.36**).

   The cell margins change.

3. (Optional) If you don't like the cell margin presets, choose Custom Margins from the Cell Margins pop-up menu.

   The Cell Text Layout dialog appears (**Figure 8.37**). Make changes in this dialog as needed, then click OK to lock in the settings.

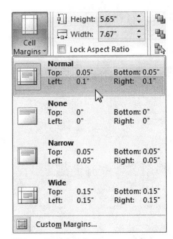

Figure 8.36 Set the amount of space within cells with the Cell Margins pop-up menu.

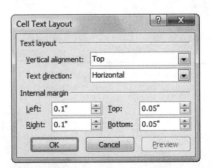

Figure 8.37 Fine tune the cell margins in this dialog.

Adding Cell Backgrounds and Graphics

Once you have set the overall table style, you can dress it up further. PowerPoint allows you to change the background color or texture for individual cells or for the whole table.

Filling cells with a background image is an excellent way to help give your table a slick, professional look. PowerPoint gives you four choices for cell backgrounds:

- **Shading** puts a solid color in the cell background.

- **Picture** puts an image in the cell background, shrinking the image to fit. You'll also use this option for images you wish to place in a cell.

- **Gradient** puts a smooth color blend in the cell background.

- **Texture** puts an image into the cell background, but in contrast to the Picture background, tiles the image to fill the cell.

The benefit of using one of these background choices is that they will move with the table and adjust their positions within cells when you resize the table, which can save you a tremendous amount of time.

Cells (or the whole table) can also have *effects*, which are bevels, shadows, and reflections that make the cells stand out.

To fill cells with a color, picture, gradient, or texture:

1. Select the cell or cells you wish to fill.

2. In Table Tools > Design > Table Styles > Shading, choose the type of fill—a color, Picture, Gradient, or Texture—from the pop-up menu (**Figure 8.38**).

   Depending on your choice, you may be able to choose from a fly-out gallery. For example, Gradient gives you a variety of gradient fills from which to choose (**Figure 8.39**).

   The table cell or cells are filled.

✔ Tips

- When adding cell backgrounds, always keep in mind that the most important information in a table is the text in it, not the cell backgrounds. You don't want to add cell backgrounds that will detract from the readability of the text in the table cells. That goes for the pattern, as well as the color, of the cell background. Remember that the data in the table needs to be easily read by the people in the back row of the auditorium.

- Make sure that the cell backgrounds complement, rather than clash, with the rest of the slide. Again, you should evaluate patterns, as well as the colors.

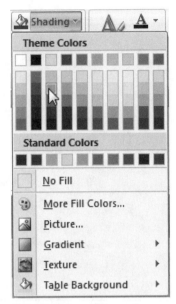

Figure 8.38 You can choose four kinds of cell fills for tables, including Colors, Picture, Gradient, or Texture.

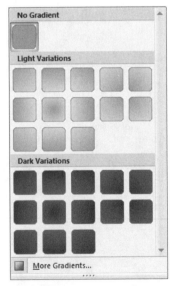

Figure 8.39 You can choose from many gradient presets.

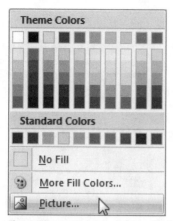

Figure 8.40 Set a color or picture for the table background in the Table Background fly-out menu.

To apply a color or picture to a table background:

1. Select the table you wish to fill.

2. Choose Table Tools > Design > Table Styles > Shading > Table Background (Figure 8.38), then choose a color or picture from the fly-out menu (**Figure 8.40**).

   If you chose Picture, the Insert Picture dialog appears. Navigate to the picture you want, select it, then click Open.

   The color or picture you chose appears as the table background (**Figure 8.41**).

✔ Tip

■ If your table has a header row, the background will not appear in that row; instead, its background color will be the default style for the table.

Division	Q1	Q2	Q3	Q4	Goal%
North	$162	$141	$148	$152	-5%
East	$120	$117	$116	$121	-7%
West	$152	$149	$144	$146	-2%
South	$110	$112	$111	$113	+1%
Pacific Rim	$14	$14	$15	$15	+12%
Asia	$9	$11	$14	$13	+10%
India	$1	$2	$1.5	$2	n/a
Europe	$91	$94	$93	$92	+2%
Canada	$26	$28	$30	$34	+11%

Figure 8.41 The image that appeared in this table did not appear in the top row, because it is set to be a header row.

ADDING CELL BACKGROUNDS AND GRAPHICS

To apply cell effects:

1. Select a cell, range of cells, or the whole table.

2. Choose Table Tools > Design > Table Styles > Effects, then choose an effect from the pop-up menu (**Figure 8.42**). The effect is applied to the table.

3. (Optional) To modify the effect, right-click the table, then choose Format Shape from the shortcut menu. In the Format Shape dialog that appears, adjust the effect to your liking (**Figure 8.43**). When you're done, click Close.

✔ Tip

■ Choosing Shadow Options from the pop-up menu in Figure 8.42 is another way to open the Format Shape dialog, set to the Shadow category, as in Figure 8.43.

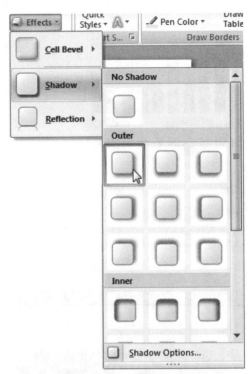

Figure 8.42 This effect will apply a drop shadow to the entire table.

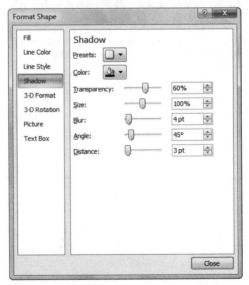

Figure 8.43 Use the Format Shape dialog to further refine your effect.

CREATING CHARTS

Charts can help viewers of your presentation better understand quantitative information without overwhelming them with an avalanche of numbers. Using a chart, you can present complex data that can be understood at a glance. Charts illustrate the relationships between different sets of data, and they are also good for showing trends over time.

PowerPoint provides you with a wide variety of chart types, and you can manipulate those charts in many different ways to get your point across. You should have no problems tailoring charts to suit your taste and the needs of your presentation.

You can also animate the parts of a chart to have them appear on your slide one at a time. To create these chart builds, see Chapter 10.

In this chapter, you'll learn about the different chart types; how to use PowerPoint to create charts; and how to manipulate those charts so that they look the way you want.

About Chart Types

PowerPoint can create eleven different types of charts, as shown in **Table 9.1**. Each type of chart is useful for displaying a particular kind of data.

It's not always easy to decide on which kind of chart to use. Sometimes the data that you're trying to present will practically beg for a particular chart type; for example, when you're trying to show values as percentages that add up to 100%, a pie chart is almost always the right approach. But in other instances, several chart types might fit your data and do a good job of presenting it. Here are a few tips to help you choose the right chart for the job.

◆ Evaluate the data that you are trying to present, particularly the aspect of the data that you want to highlight. Data where the totals are more important than the individual values are good candidates for area charts, stacked bar charts, and stacked column charts.

◆ If you have many data series to present, use a chart type like bar, column, or X Y (Scatter), which shows many data points well.

◆ Choose the chart type that produces the simplest chart for your data. If necessary, switch between the different types in PowerPoint to see the visual effect of each type on the data. Because your viewers don't have control of how long your slide is on screen, it will help if you give them charts they can grasp quickly.

◆ Pie charts shouldn't be used to represent data with more than five to eight data series. Each series will appear as a slice of the pie, and too-small pieces will not have good visual impact.

Table 9.1

Chart Types	
CHART TYPE	DESCRIPTION
Column	Column charts show unique values. They are useful when comparing values, such as sales, over different time periods. Stacked column charts, like area charts, display both individual values and the sum of several values for a given item.
Line	Line charts show data trends over time or other intervals. They are useful for showing variations in values, such as stock prices.
Pie	Pie charts show proportional relationships between several values and a whole, often expressed as percentages.
Bar	Bar charts, like column charts, show individual items and their relationship to one another. The stacked bar chart variation is similar to the stacked column chart.
Area	Area charts show the magnitude of change over time. A variation, stacked area charts, also shows the magnitude of change over time, and they display both individual values and the sum of all values in the chart.
X Y (Scatter)	Scatter charts are often used for scientific data, and plot two groups of numbers as one series of xy coordinates, or shows the relationships among the numeric values in several data series.
Stock	These are usually used to plot stock price data, and show the high, low, and closing prices of one or more stocks.
Surface	Surface charts display data plotted over a 3D surface area, and compare two groups of data combinations. Similar colors and patterns indicate similar ranges of values.
Doughnut	Similar to a pie chart, except that it can show more than one data series. Like the pie chart, it shows the proportion of parts to the whole.
Bubble	A variation of the XY chart, this chart compares sets of three values. The size of the bubble indicates the value of the third variable.
Radar	The radar chart compares multiple data series that are all related to a single item.

Chart anatomy

Before you begin creating charts, you'll need to know a little about the terminology PowerPoint uses to refer to the different parts of a chart, and the different tools that PowerPoint gives you to manipulate charts. The column chart in **Figure 9.1** labels the main parts that appear on a slide. PowerPoint uses Excel 2007 to enter the information that makes up the chart (**Figure 9.2**, on the following page). Data behind the chart is entered in an Excel worksheet. When you have selected a chart in PowerPoint, the Chart Tools contextual tabs (Design, Layout, and Format) appear in the Ribbon, which gives you many controls that allow you to customize the chart (**Figure 9.3**, on the following page).

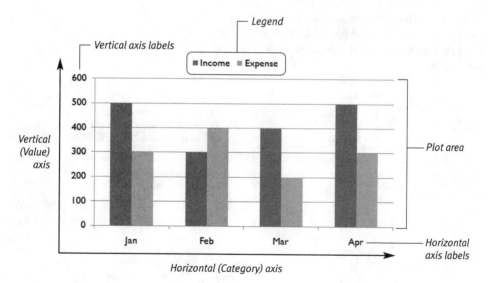

Figure 9.1 The parts of a column chart.

The data for the chart appears in the *plot area*, which contains the bars, columns, lines, etc. Most chart types (except for pie, doughnut, and radar charts) have two axes, the horizontal *category axis* and the vertical *value axis*. The value axis is where you read the values you are charting. For example, in Figure 9.1, the value axis is the vertical axis, the one with the numeric labels. In column charts, area charts, and line charts, the vertical axis is the value axis. For bar charts, the horizontal axis is the value axis, and the vertical axis is the category axis. Pie, doughnut, and radar charts don't have a value axis.

Charts show the relationship between two types of data (for example, financial performance over a time period such as months or years). These two data types are called the *data series* and *data sets*. In Figure 9.2, each row in the worksheet represents a data series, and each column represents a data set. The *legend* is the label (or labels) on the chart that explains what the different data series represent.

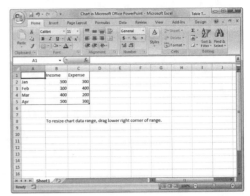

Figure 9.2 The Excel worksheet contains the data for your chart.

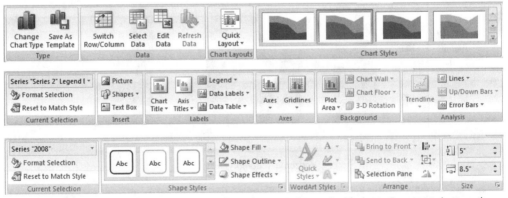

Figure 9.3 The Chart Tools contextual tabs give you the tools you need to work with charts. From top to bottom, they are the Design, Layout, and Format tabs.

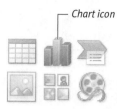

Chart icon

Figure 9.4 Click the Chart icon in the content box to get started creating a chart.

Figure 9.5 For slide layouts without a content box, use the Insert tab to start your chart.

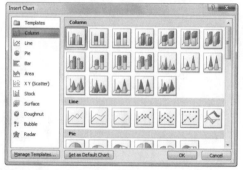

Figure 9.6 The Insert Chart dialog gives you access to dozens of predefined chart types.

Adding Charts

You'll want to add a chart to a slide that has plenty of room for the chart, though you can add a chart to any slide, especially slides that have a content box. Of the built-in slide layouts, the ones that are most appropriate for charts are Title and Content, Two Content, Comparison, Content with Caption, Title Only, and of course Blank, which is a good layout to use for charts that need to be as large as possible.

To add a chart to a slide:

1. Display the slide where you want to add a chart.

2. If your layout has a content box, click the Chart icon (**Figure 9.4**).

   or

   Choose Insert > Illustrations > Chart (**Figure 9.5**).

   The Insert Chart dialog appears (**Figure 9.6**).

3. Choose the chart type that you want from the category on the left, then choose a chart style in the scrolling list on the right.

   continues on next page

ADDING CHARTS

4. Click OK.

Excel 2007 launches, with some sample data already entered. Surrounding the sample data is a border delineating the *chart data range* (**Figure 9.7**). The row and column labels and the data within this border will appear on the chart.

5. Enter your data into the Excel worksheet.

For more information about using the worksheet, see the next section.

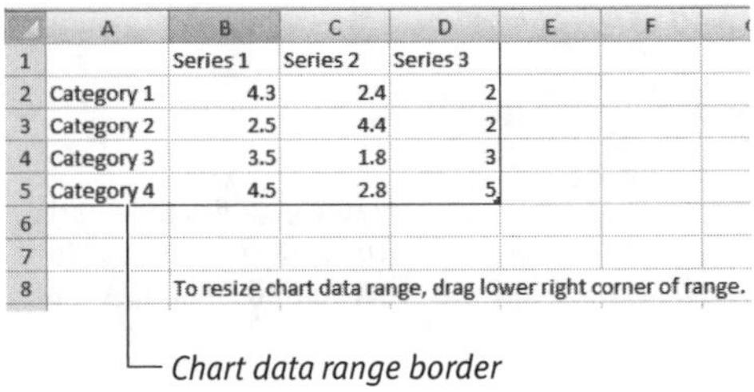

✔ Tips

■ If you already have an Excel worksheet with your data, you can create the chart in Excel, then copy the chart and paste it into PowerPoint. There won't be any difference in the look of the chart versus creating it in both Excel and PowerPoint.

■ You can add as many charts as you want to a slide, subject only to how many will fit on the slide, and to your sense of good taste.

	A	B	C	D	E	F	
1		Series 1	Series 2	Series 3			
2	Category 1	4.3	2.4	2			
3	Category 2	2.5	4.4	2			
4	Category 3	3.5	1.8	3			
5	Category 4	4.5	2.8	5			
6							
7							
8			To resize chart data range, drag lower right corner of range.				

— Chart data range border

Figure 9.7 To expand or reduce the plot area, drag the chart data range border.

When Excel is Missing

Almost always, if you have PowerPoint 2007 installed, you will also have Excel 2007 on your computer, and PowerPoint will use Excel as the spreadsheet behind charts that you create. But it's possible to have PowerPoint without the rest of the Office 2007 suite, and in that case, when you create a chart, a separate program called Microsoft Graph appears.

Graph is a "legacy" program, meaning that it is only included in the Office 2007 installation for compatibility purposes. In fact, you can't even start Graph unless Excel isn't present.

Graph does not have the improved charting graphics engine of the main Office 2007 programs, so charts that you create with Graph won't look the same (or as good) as charts shown in this book.

◢	A	B	C	D
1		Series 1	Series 2	Series 3
2	Category 1	4.3	2.4	2
3	Category 2	2.5	4.4	2
4	Category 3	3.5	1.8	3
5	Category 4	4.5	2.8	5

Figure 9.8 You'll need to highlight the sample data in the worksheet before you can delete it.

Figure 9.9 You can use the Ribbon or the keyboard to delete the sample data in the worksheet.

A	B	C
	Series 1	Series 2
Category 1		
Category 2		

A	B	C
	2007	Series 2
Category 1		
Category 2		
Category 3		

Figure 9.10 First you highlight one of the labels in the worksheet (top), and then you type in the new label (bottom).

Using Excel to Enter Chart Data

When you create a new chart in PowerPoint, the Excel worksheet is filled by default with four rows and three columns of sample data. Chances are this won't be the data that you want, so the first thing you'll need to do is get rid of the sample data so that you don't accidentally mistake it for your own data. Next, you'll need to change the row and column labels so that they match your chart's data. After that, you can enter your data in the Excel worksheet's cells.

Once your data is in place, you can rearrange it by moving rows or columns around on the worksheet, and you can even choose parts of the worksheet data to include in the chart.

To delete all data in the Excel worksheet:

1. Click and drag over the sample data in the worksheet to highlight it (**Figure 9.8**).

2. Choose Home > Editing > Clear, then from the pop-up menu, choose Clear Contents (**Figure 9.9**).

   or

   Press Delete.

   The values in the selected cells disappear.

To change row or column labels:

1. In the worksheet, click the name of the row or column that you want to change.

   The cell containing the name is highlighted (**Figure 9.10**).

2. Type the new name.

   The new name replaces the old.

3. Click outside the label to accept the change.

To enter data in the worksheet:

1. Click a cell in the worksheet, then type.

2. Press the Tab key to complete the entry and move the selection to the right.

   See **Table 9.2** for more ways to enter data and move the selection in the worksheet.

3. (Optional) If you need another row, click in the last cell of the worksheet, then press Tab.

   or

   Drag the handle at the lower-right corner of the chart data range to the right (to add a column) or down (to add a row).

   The chart data range expands.

To move rows or columns:

1. In the worksheet, click one of the row or column headers to select the row or column.

   The row or column highlights.

2. Choose Home > Clipboard > Cut, or press Ctrl X.

   The selected area shows a border with a moving dotted line.

3. Click where you want to move the highlighted cells.

4. Choose Home > Cells > Insert > Insert Cut Cells.

   The row or column moves.

✔ Tip

- You must insert the cut cells within the chart data area. If you do not, Excel will show an error message.

Table 9.2

Chart Data Entry Shortcuts

KEY	WHAT IT DOES
Tab	Completes a cell entry and moves the selection to the right
Shift-Tab	Completes a cell entry and moves the selection to the left
Enter	Completes a cell entry and moves the selection down
Shift-Enter	Completes a cell entry and moves the selection up
Home	Moves the selection to the beginning of the row
Arrow Keys	Moves the selection one cell in the direction of the arrow

USING EXCEL TO ENTER CHART DATA

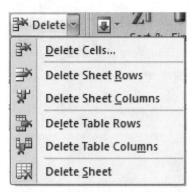

Figure 9.11 You have a variety of deletion options in the Delete pop-up menu.

To resize columns in the worksheet:

1. Position the mouse pointer over the boundary between two of the column labels.

   The cursor will change into a double-headed arrow.

2. Click and drag right or left to increase or decrease the column's width.

To delete a row or column:

1. Click a row or column label to select an entire row or column.

2. Choose Home > Cells > Delete, then choose the action you want from the Delete pop-up menu (**Figure 9.11**).

   or

   Move the mouse pointer over the selected data, then right-click to bring up the shortcut menu, then choose Delete.

   The row or column disappears.

To hide or unhide a row or column:

1. If you have data in your worksheet that you don't want to be part of the chart, you can hide it. Begin by selecting the row or column you want to hide.

2. Right-click and choose Hide from the shortcut menu.

   The row or column disappears, and the chart in PowerPoint changes to reflect the new data, recalculating totals and other data as needed.

3. To unhide the row or column, select the rows and columns before and after the hidden row or column. Then right-click and choose Unhide.

USING EXCEL TO ENTER CHART DATA

Changing Chart Types

You can change the chart type at any time in PowerPoint. All you need to do is select the chart and then choose from the Type group in the Chart Tools or use the shortcut menu.

To change the chart type:

1. Select a chart.

2. Right-click and choose Change Chart Type from the shortcut menu (**Figure 9.12**).

   or

   Choose Chart Tools > Design > Type > Change Chart Type.

   The Change Chart Type dialog appears, which looks just like Figure 9.6 with a different window title.

3. Choose the chart type that you want from the category on the left, then choose a chart style in the scrolling list on the right.

4. Click OK.

   The chart changes. The options in the Ribbon's Chart Tools tabs also change to show options appropriate to the new chart types.

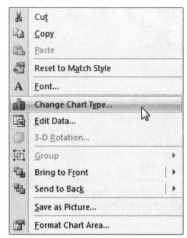

Figure 9.12 It's often faster to use the shortcut menu rather than the Ribbon.

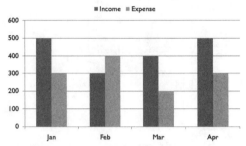

Figure 9.13 The rows in the worksheet represent the data series.

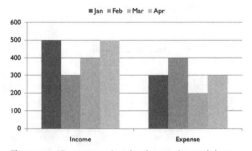

Figure 9.14 When charted, the data series group the financial data together by month.

Figure 9.15 By transposing the data series and data sets, you see all the income and all the expense figures grouped together.

Transposing Chart Plots

Sometimes you need to look at your data in a different way, and PowerPoint can transpose the way it plots the data series and data sets, to give you a different perspective on your data.

In the example in **Figure 9.13**, the rows (data series) in the worksheet show income and expense figures distributed across four months, which are expressed in the columns (data sets). The resulting graph (**Figure 9.14**) groups each month's financial results together. If we transpose the data series and data sets, we get a very different view of the same data (**Figure 9.15**). In this view, you can see how income and expenses change over the four months. The income figures and the expense figures for all months are grouped together, making it easier to see the trend for each group over time. PowerPoint changes the legend of the graph to reflect the new ordering of the data.

The benefit of being able to transpose data series and data sets is that it allows you to change the presentation of the data in the worksheet without the need to retype your data.

To transpose data series and data sets:

1. Select a chart on a slide.

2. Choose Chart Tools > Design > Data > Switch Row/Column (**Figure 9.16**).
   The chart changes.

Figure 9.16 Use the Switch Row/Column button to transpose data sets.

Setting Chart Style and Layout

Like most other objects in PowerPoint, charts appear with a default style that matches the presentation's theme. A *chart style* is a combination that includes the chart's fonts and colors, and also effects, such as 3-D, shadow, or beveled effects on the parts of the chart. As usual with PowerPoint 2007, you are able to pick different chart styles from a gallery.

PowerPoint also includes 11 different preset *chart layouts*. A chart layout is a set of chart elements with a particular arrangement. For example, one layout includes a chart title, with the legend at the right side of the chart. Another one puts the legend above the chart, and also includes a data table that shows all of the values that are normally hidden in the worksheet.

To change the chart style:

1. Select the chart on your slide.

2. Choose one of the styles in the Chart Tools > Design > Chart Styles gallery (**Figure 9.17**).

   The style is applied to your chart.

3. (Optional) If you want to see all of the styles available, click the More button in the Chart Styles gallery.

   The gallery expands to show you all the choices. Click one of the styles to apply it to your chart.

To apply a chart layout:

1. Select the chart on your slide.

2. Choose one of the styles in the Chart Tools > Design > Chart Layouts gallery (**Figure 9.18**).

   The chart takes on the layout you chose (**Figure 9.19**).

More button ⌐

Figure 9.17 The Chart Styles gallery has dozens of preset styles.

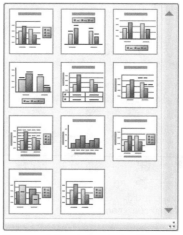

Figure 9.18 The choices in the Chart Layouts gallery are a great start for formatting your charts.

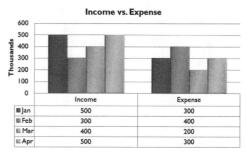

Figure 9.19 This chart layout includes the data table, as well as the chart.

✔ Tip

■ Unlike most of the other galleries in PowerPoint, the galleries for Chart Styles and Chart Layouts do not provide live previews as you hover your mouse pointer over a possible layout or style.

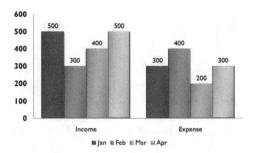

Figure 9.20 I used the Fonts group in the Home tab to increase the size of the labels on the value axis and make them boldface.

Modifying Chart Elements

You can format the different parts of a chart to serve your needs. You can change the chart's colors, fonts, gridlines, legend, and axis labels and control the formatting of numbers in charts.

You'll use the Chart Tools tabs to make most of the formatting changes to your charts.

Changing colors and fonts

There's not much difference between the text and graphics on a chart and any other text and graphic objects in PowerPoint. You select the item you wish to change, then use the same kinds of tools to make the modifications as you would any similar text or graphic.

You change chart colors as you would any graphic, and you can apply image, gradient, or color fills, change the opacity, add shadows, and change the line styles.

For more details about working with text, see Chapter 4; for more about working with graphics, see Chapter 5.

To change text in charts:

1. Select the text that you wish to change.

    You can select several text boxes in each chart: the chart title, the legend, the data point labels (if they are visible), the category axis label, and the value axis label.

2. Use the tools in the Fonts and Paragraph groups of the Home tab of the Ribbon to adjust the appearance of the text (**Figure 9.20**).

To change graphics in charts:

1. Select the graphic element that you wish to change.

   In bar and column charts, if you select one element in a series, all the elements in that series are selected (**Figure 9.21**). In a pie chart, you can select one or more wedges of the pie.

2. Use the graphics tools in the Chart Tools > Format > Shape Styles group to adjust the fill, outline, shadow, or other effects of the selected object or objects (**Figure 9.22**).

To remove formatting:

1. Sometimes you may want to restore the chart to the default theme style. Begin by selecting the chart.

2. Choose Chart Tools > Layout > Current Selection > Reset to Match Style.

   Any style modifications you've made are eliminated, and the chart returns to its default style.

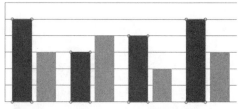

Figure 9.21 Selecting one of the elements in a series selects all of the elements of that series.

Figure 9.22 Use the Shape Styles group to change the graphic look of objects.

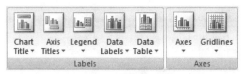

Figure 9.23 Many different parts of a chart have labels, and you modify them with the Labels group.

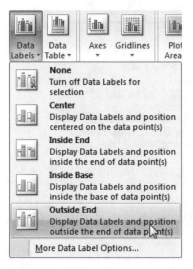

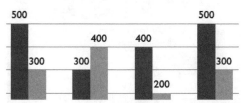

Figure 9.24 The icons in the Data Labels pop-up menu give you an idea what the effect will look like (top), and then the numeric values in the worksheet appear in the chart (bottom).

Modifying axis elements

Axis elements include the labels for the category axis and value axis, gridlines, the range of values that are displayed along the value axis, and the number format of the values in the chart. You can also adjust the borders of the chart. You'll find the controls for these settings in the Labels and Axes groups of the Layout tab of Chart Tools (**Figure 9.23**).

To change chart and axis labels:

1. Select the chart.

2. In the Labels group of the Layout tab of Chart Tools, make one or more selections from the pop-up menus for the element you want to change.

   The pop-up menus are different for each kind of element. For example, to add data labels to each chart element, you can choose where you want to position the data labels (**Figure 9.24**).

   As you make changes to the pop-up menus, the chart changes.

✔ Tip

■ Column and Stacked Column charts usually look better without gridlines in the X-axis, and with gridlines turned on in the Y-axis. The reverse is true for Bar and Stacked Bar charts. Line charts often look good with gridlines turned on for both axes.

To change the range of displayed values on the value axis:

1. Select the chart.

2. Choose Chart Tools > Layout, then choose Vertical (Value) Axis from the Chart Elements pop-up menu at the top of the Current Selection group (**Figure 9.25**).

    The vertical axis will be selected.

3. Choose Chart Tools > Layout > Current Selection > Format Selection.

    The Format Axis dialog appears, set to the Axis Options category (**Figure 9.26**).

4. Choose one or more of the following:

    ▲ In the Minimum field, click the Fixed button, then enter a number.

    This number will be the value that will be shown at the *chart origin*, which is where the category axis and the value axis meet.

    ▲ In the Maximum field, click the Fixed button, then enter a number.

    This will be the highest number displayed on the value axis label. It must be as high as or higher than the highest value in your data set.

    ▲ Click the Fixed button, then enter values for the Major unit and Minor unit fields.

    This creates marks in the value axis with values at equal intervals. The more steps that you specify, the more axis markings there will be.

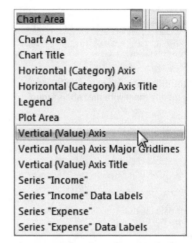

Figure 9.25 The Chart Elements pop-up menu is the easiest way to make sure that you've selected the right part of the chart.

Figure 9.26 You can change the numeric range in the value axis in this dialog.

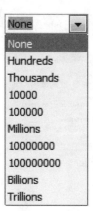

Figure 9.27 Making a choice from this pop-up menu will place a corresponding units label in the chart.

Figure 9.28 Use the Number category of the Format Axis dialog to fine tune numeric display in your chart.

▲ Select the Values in reverse order or Logarithmic scale checkboxes. The latter works best when your chart values cover a large range.

▲ If you want to show units in the chart, make a selection from the Display units pop-up menu (**Figure 9.27**).

5. When you're done modifying the axis display, click Close.

✔ Tip

■ Choosing even numbers as your maximum and unit values will make for clean labels on the value axis. If the maximum value isn't easily divisible by the unit value, PowerPoint displays numbers with decimals.

To set the number format of chart values:

1. Select the chart.

2. Choose Chart Tools > Layout, then choose Vertical (Value) Axis from the Chart Elements pop-up menu at the top of the Current Selection group.
The vertical axis will be selected.

3. Choose Chart Tools > Layout > Current Selection > Format Selection.
The Format Axis dialog appears.

4. Click the Number category.
The dialog displays the Number options (**Figure 9.28**).

continues on next page

5. Choose a number category from the list. The dialog changes to show different options, depending on the category you pick.

6. Make the number formatting changes you want.

7. Click Close.

✔ Tip

■ If you arrange the Format Axis dialog and the PowerPoint window correctly, you can see changes you make to number formats reflected in the chart as you make them, allowing you to do the formatting more efficiently.

To format axes and gridlines:

1. Select the chart.

2. In the Axes group of the Layout tab of the Chart Tools, make one or more selections from the pop-up menus for the element you want to change.

Each of the two pop-up menus—Axes and Gridlines—has Horizontal and Vertical submenus, with several options for each one (**Figure 9.29**).

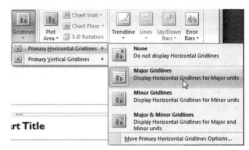

Figure 9.29 You can adjust the horizontal and vertical gridlines settings separately.

Working with Pie Charts

Pie charts work a bit differently than the other charts in PowerPoint. Because a pie chart doesn't have a category axis and a value axis, PowerPoint charts only the first data set in the worksheet. If the data series are in rows in the worksheet, only the first column will be charted. If the data series are in columns in the worksheet, only the first row will be charted. A single pie chart represents a single data set, and each wedge in the pie chart represents one element of that set. If there are other data sets in the worksheet, and you switch the chart type to a pie chart, the excess data sets will not disappear, but they will not be used, either.

PowerPoint allows you to manipulate the individual wedges of a pie chart separately. You can select a wedge and manually drag it away from the main body of the pie chart for effect, or you can use a slider to "explode" a wedge of the chart if you like, separating it from the rest of the chart by a specified percentage. You can also rotate an entire pie chart, to show off a particular part.

✔ Tip

■ You can chart any data set that is in your worksheet by moving it to the first position in its row or column.

To select pie wedges:

1. Select the chart.

2. Double-click to select a single wedge.

To explode a pie chart:

1. Select a pie wedge.

2. Drag the wedge away from the rest of the pie (**Figure 9.30**).

    or

    To explode all of the wedges away from one another, right click the pie chart and choose Format Data Series from the shortcut menu (**Figure 9.31**).

    The Format Data Series dialog appears.

3. In the Pie Explosion section, use the slider or the numeric field to explode the pie segments, then click Close.

    The wedges separate from one another (**Figure 9.32**).

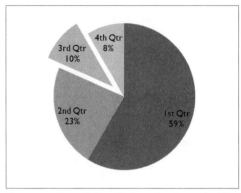

Figure 9.30 To explode a single wedge, just select it and drag it away from the rest of the chart.

Figure 9.31 The Pie Explosion slider lets you move the wedges apart.

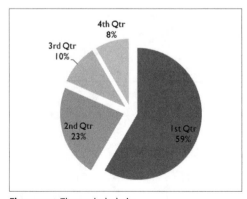

Figure 9.32 The exploded pie.

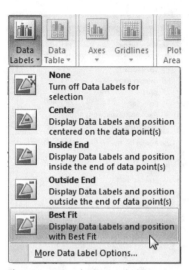

Figure 9.33 Use the Data Labels menu to turn on and position data labels.

To show and format values in pie wedges:

1. Select the chart.

2. In Chart Tools > Layout > Labels, select a label format from the Data Labels pop-up menu (**Figure 9.33**).

   This turns on the value labels for each data point in the chart (**Figure 9.34**).

continues on next page

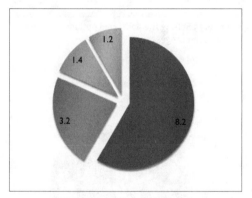

Figure 9.34 These data labels are the same values in the Excel worksheet. They need more work to show as percentages.

WORKING WITH PIE CHARTS

3. To format the data value labels, right-click the pie and choose Format Data Labels from the shortcut menu.

The Format Data Labels dialog appears (**Figure 9.35**).

4. Make changes in this dialog as needed, then click Close.

The data labels are formatted as you command (**Figure 9.36**).

✔ Tip

■ You can select and set font styles for each data point label separately. This allows you to do things like increase the font size and change the color of the label inside an exploded wedge, further highlighting that wedge.

Figure 9.35 Setting the data label options, displayed here as percentages.

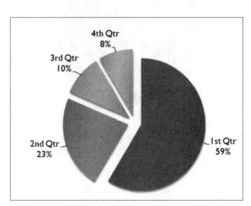

Figure 9.36 The finished data labels.

Resizing Charts

You resize any kind of chart as you would any other graphic object in PowerPoint.

To resize a chart:

1. Select the chart.

   Selection handles appear at the chart's edges.

2. Click and drag one of the selection handles.

   The chart resizes. Charts always resize proportionately.

Saving Charts as Templates

When you've spent a lot of time formatting a chart, you don't want to reinvent it every time you need that format. PowerPoint lets you save charts as templates. Instead of re-creating the chart, you can simply apply the chart template.

To save a chart as a template:

1. Select the chart that you want to save as a template.

2. Choose Chart Tools > Design > Type > Save As Template (**Figure 9.37**).

   The Save Chart Template dialog appears, set to save the template in the template folder where PowerPoint expects to find templates. Don't change this.

3. Give the template a name, and click OK.

   PowerPoint saves the template.

To apply a saved chart template:

1. Select a chart on your slide.

2. Choose Chart Tools > Design > Type > Change Chart Type.

   The Change Chart Type dialog appears.

3. Click Templates, select the previously saved template (**Figure 9.38**), and then click OK.

   The chart takes on the formatting of your chart template.

Figure 9.37 When you save a chart template, you can save yourself a lot of future work.

Figure 9.38 Choose the template you previously saved to apply it to a chart on your slide.

USING SLIDE TRANSITIONS AND ANIMATIONS

10

Once you have written your presentation and pulled together all the text and graphics that will go into the presentation you should review the show, and if needed, reorganize your slides the way you like them. Then you can add motion and visual appeal to your slideshow with slide transitions and animations.

Slide transitions are animated effects that occur when you switch from one slide to another. Transitions between slides can enhance the effect of your presentation and help your audience by clearly marking when you're done with a slide (and also, presumably letting them know that you're moving from one topic to the next). An *animation effect* is the generic name for an animation that occurs within the body of the slide, and PowerPoint 2007 makes it easier to add animation to your slides. Some animations involve one or more elements of an object, and you can control how objects animate onto the slide and how they leave the slide. For example, you can have the parts of a graph appear on the screen one at a time (called a *chart animation*), or make text boxes or graphics fly onto (or off of) the screen. *Text animations* are used for animating the way that different lines of bulleted text appear on the slide.

In this chapter, you'll learn how to use PowerPoint's Slide Sorter; apply slide transitions; and create the different types of object animations.

Using the Slide Sorter

As you've been developing your presentation, especially during the writing phase, you've seen how the topic of one slide flows into the next, and perhaps that flow is perfect for your show. But maybe the presentation would be a bit better, a touch tighter, if you moved that slide there, and moved that other slide over here. PowerPoint's Slide Sorter View shows you many slides at once, and allows you to drag one or more slides to other places in the presentation. Slide Sorter View also offers a convenient way to apply slide transitions to multiple slides in one operation (you'll see how to do that later in this chapter).

Figure 10.1 Open Slide Sorter View with this button in the Ribbon.

Figure 10.2 You can also use the button at the bottom of the PowerPoint window to get into Slide Sorter View.

To rearrange slides in Slide Sorter View:

1. Choose View > Presentation Views > Slide Sorter (**Figure 10.1**).

   or

   Click the Slide Sorter View button at the bottom of the PowerPoint window (**Figure 10.2**).

   The PowerPoint window switches to Slide Sorter View (**Figure 10.3**).

2. Click the slide you want to move, then drag it to the new location.

   As you drag, the slide indicator line shows you where the slide will go when you release the mouse button (**Figure 10.4**).

USING THE SLIDE SORTER

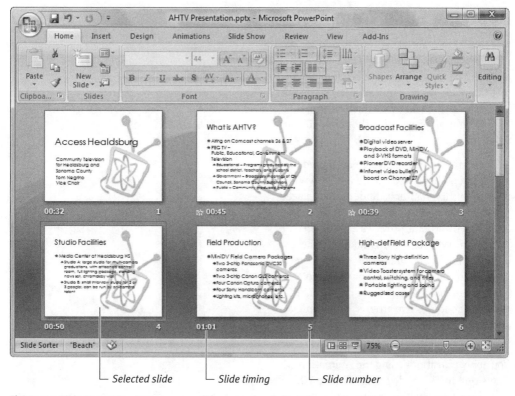

Figure 10.3 Slide Sorter View lets you move slides around and also tells you other information about the slides.

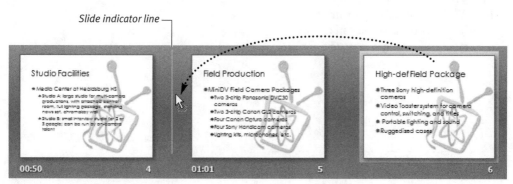

Figure 10.4 Drag the slide to its new location.

USING THE SLIDE SORTER

Applying Slide Transitions

Slide transitions are a good way to add visual interest when you change slides. They also serve as a cue to the audience, reinforcing the fact that you are changing slides; if someone isn't paying particularly close attention, that flash of motion often helps them refocus on your slideshow.

All slide transitions involve an animated effect where the first, old slide (which I will refer to in this chapter as Slide A) is replaced by the second, new slide (you guessed it, Slide B). PowerPoint provides 58 built-in transition styles, plus No Transition. These are 2-D transitions, where one slide replaces another in the same plane. For example, Slide A can dissolve into Slide B. The transitions are split into five groups: Fades and Dissolves, Wipes, Push and Cover, Stripes and Bars, and Random.

You apply transitions using the Animations > Transition to This Slide group (**Figure 10.5**). You can set a transition between any two or more slides (they must be contiguous in the Normal View pane or the Slide Sorter, of course). You can control (to a point) the speed of a transition, and you can choose to have a sound accompany the transition.

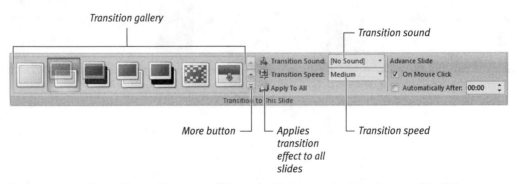

Transition gallery

Transition sound

More button — Applies transition effect to all slides

Transition speed

Figure 10.5 Most of your slide transition needs will be met by this group on the Animations tab of the Ribbon.

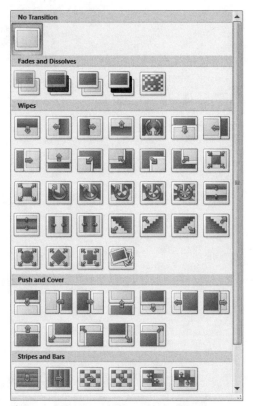

Figure 10.6 The expanded Transition gallery shows you all the possible transitions (most of which you'll probably never use).

With slide transitions, as with any animation and PowerPoint, you should live by the principle "less is more" when choosing transitions, because the flashier they are, the more quickly your audience will become tired of them. The most common transition, Fade Smoothly, is often the most effective.

To apply a slide transition:

1. Switch to Slide Sorter View by clicking the Slide Show View button at the bottom of the PowerPoint window, or choose View > Presentation Views > Slide Sorter.

   The PowerPoint window changes to Slide Sorter View.

2. Select the slide or slides to which you want to apply the transition.

   To select multiple slides, click the first slide, hold down the Shift key, and click the last slide.

   Those slides and all slides in between are selected.

   or

   To select all the slides easily, press Ctrl A.

3. Choose Animations > Transition to This Slide, then choose a transition effect from the Transition gallery.

   The effect is applied to the selected slides. As usual with galleries, you'll see a preview of the effect on the slide as you hover your mouse over effect thumbnails in the gallery.

4. (Optional) To expand the gallery and see more effects, click the gallery's More button.

   The gallery expands (**Figure 10.6**).

   continues on next page

APPLYING SLIDE TRANSITIONS

5. Choose the speed of the transition by selecting it from the Transition Speed pop-up menu. Your choices are Slow, Medium, and Fast. The default speed is Fast.

6. (Optional) Choose a sound from the Transition Sound pop-up menu.

   This sound will play between each of the selected slides. Use it sparingly, if at all; many audiences hate sound effects in presentations.

7. In the Advance Slide section, choose On Mouse Click if you want to trigger the transition manually while running the presentation (this is what you usually will want).

   or

   Choose Automatically After if you want the transition to occur by itself. You must also set the delay in minutes and seconds; this specifies how long the slide will stay on the screen before triggering the transition.

8. (Optional) By default, the transition you chose is applied only to the slide you selected in Step 2. Click the Apply To All button to add the transition to the entire presentation.

Less Really Is More

When it comes to slide transitions, restraint really should be the order of the day. Chances are you've seen presentations where presenters used way too many transitions and animated effects. Did you like them? No? That's what I thought.

Too-busy slide transitions and animations of objects on the slide can easily distract the audience from the content of your presentation. Make sure not to overdo them, or you might find your audience slipping out of the room before your talk is over—which is not the sign of a successful presentation. Too much swooping and spinning can even make some audience members nauseous!

✔ Tips

- You can use slide transitions to communicate different types of information or to denote sections in your presentation. For example, you can use a transition to signify that you're moving to an entirely different topic in your presentation. Let's say that you have a presentation with three distinct sections. You can use no transitions between the slides in each section, and use transitions only between slides at the end of one section and the beginning of the next.

- PowerPoint lets you set almost any length for automatic transitions (I don't know just what the upper limit is, but it accepted 100 hours between automatic slide changes, which would make for a pretty languid slideshow).

- PowerPoint doesn't allow you to create your own transition styles. You are limited to the ones that come with the program. You can also purchase additional transitions (as well as other PowerPoint add-ins) from software developers, such as CrystalGraphics (www.crystalgraphics.com).

- You're not limited to the transition sounds shown in the pop-up menu in Step 6. If you want to use one of your own sounds, choose Other Sound from that pop-up menu, which opens the Add Sound dialog box. Navigate to and select the sound you want to use, and click OK.

Applying Animation Effects

You've seen animation effects in most presentations; these are the effects that are responsible for titles, bulleted text, charts, or diagrams that fade, wipe, or animate onto the screen when the presenter clicks the mouse button. PowerPoint has two ways to apply animations to objects on your slides. The first way is to use the preset animation effects. These are basic animation schemes with common effects for the different sorts of slide objects. For example, the basic animation effects for bulleted text allow you to wipe or fade text onto the screen one line at a time, or in groups by first-level paragraphs. Similarly, the effects for charts include the ability to animate each of the elements on the chart.

Probably the most common sort of animation you will be doing is with bulleted text, to make each bullet and its associated text appear when you click the mouse button during the presentation. These text animations can be set up with a number of options so that you can control how the text appears on the slide. To set these options, you use the Custom Animation task pane.

To apply animation to a slide object:

1. Switch to a slide with the object you want to animate.

2. Click the bulleted text placeholder or other object to select it (**Figure 10.7**).

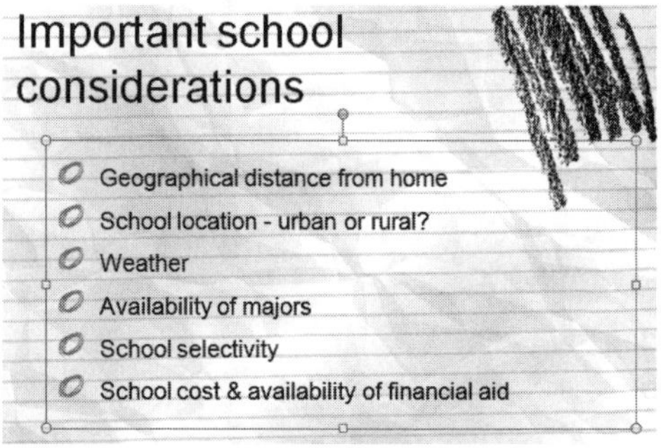

Figure 10.7 Before you can apply an animation, you must select the object. In this example, I've selected the bulleted text box.

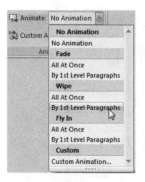

Figure 10.8 The animation presets are a good place to begin applying an animation. This menu changes, depending on the selected object. This is the menu for a bulleted text box.

Figure 10.9 Begin customizing an animation by clicking the Custom Animation button.

Figure 10.10 The Custom Animation task pane, with the top effect collapsed to just one line.

3. Choose Animations > Animations > Animate. From the pop-up menu, choose the animation preset you want (**Figure 10.8**). This pop-up menu may have a different appearance from the one shown here, depending on what object you have selected on the slide.

As you roll over the different choices in the menu, PowerPoint shows you a live preview of the effect in the slide area. To play the preview again, just move the mouse to another menu choice, then back to your original one.

The effect is applied to the slide.

To customize animation effect options:

1. Make sure the object (in this example, a bulleted text box) is selected.

2. Click Animations > Animations > Custom Animation (**Figure 10.9**).

The Custom Animation task pane opens (**Figure 10.10**).

In the list, the different bullet points are collapsed, because they all share the same effect.

continues on next page

APPLYING ANIMATION EFFECTS

3. To see all the bullet points, click the down arrow under the displayed bullet point.

The individual bullet points appear (**Figure 10.11**).

You might want to show all the bullet points so you can apply different effects to some of them.

4. By default, "On Click" is selected from the Start pop-up menu. This means that you need to click the mouse while giving your presentation in order for the animation to start. If you want the animation to begin automatically as soon as you switch to the slide, choose "After Previous" from the pop-up menu.

After you make any change in the Custom Animation task pane, PowerPoint shows you a preview of the effect in the slide area.

5. From the Direction pop-up menu, choose the direction from which you want bulleted text to move onto the slide.

6. Use the Speed pop-up menu to select the duration of the effect. Your choices are Very Slow, Slow, Medium, Fast, and Very Fast.

Figure 10.11 The expanded effect shows all of the lines in the bulleted text box.

Figure 10.12 For more control over the effect, choose Effect Options.

Figure 10.13 The Effect Options dialog changes slightly, depending on the kind of effect you're modifying.

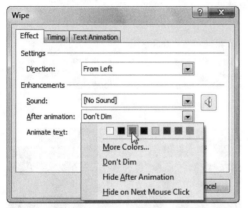

Figure 10.14 Pick a color that you want the bulleted text to change to when you move onto the next line.

7. (Optional) For more effect customizations, click the down arrow next to an item in the Custom Animation list, then choose Effect Options (**Figure 10.12**).

The Effect Options dialog appears (**Figure 10.13**). It will have the same name as the effect that you are customizing.

8. (Optional) Make any changes you want, then click OK to dismiss the Effect Options dialog.

✔ Tips

■ The effect speeds in seconds are as follows: Very Slow (5 seconds); Slow (3 seconds); Medium (2 seconds); Fast (1 second); and Very Fast (half a second).

■ A common text effect you might want is to dim one line of bulleted text when you move onto the next line. You do that in the Effect tab of the Effect Options dialog. In the Enhancements section, choose the color you want the line of text to turn to from the After animation pop-up menu (**Figure 10.14**).

APPLYING ANIMATION EFFECTS

Creating Chart Builds

Chart animations rank just behind bulleted text animations in usefulness. You can get some dramatic effects when you make the parts of a chart appear sequentially on the screen.

To animate a chart:

1. Switch to a slide with the chart you want to animate.

2. On your slide, select the chart.

3. Choose Animations > Animations > Animate. From the pop-up menu, choose the animation preset you want (**Figure 10.15**).

   Your choices are (under Fade, Wipe, or Fly In):

   ▲ **As One Object** animates the entire contents of the chart onto or off of the slide.

   ▲ **By Series** builds each data series onto or off of the slide, one at a time.

   ▲ **By Category** builds each data set onto the chart, one at a time.

   ▲ **By Element in Series** builds each element in a data series, one at a time. For example, in a chart like the one in **Figure 10.16**, the columns marked "Need requested" appear first, followed by the columns marked "Aid available."

   ▲ **By Element in Category** builds each element in a data set, one at a time.

   As you roll over the different choices in the menu, PowerPoint shows you a live preview of the effect in the slide area. When you find an effect you like, choose it from the menu.

   The effect is applied to the slide.

4. (Optional) Customize the effect as described in "To customize animation effect options" earlier in this chapter.

Figure 10.15
The animation presets for a chart.

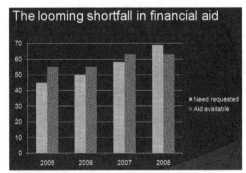

Figure 10.16 When you build chart elements by category, the columns marked "Need requested" appear before the columns marked "Aid available."

Working with Custom Animations

General object animations work much the same way as the previous animations in this chapter. The only difference is that you will be working with any element that you can place on the slide, including text boxes, charts, tables, SmartArt, or graphics.

When you are animating multiple objects, you can control the order in which those objects appear, and each object can have its own animation effect, direction, and speed. So you can, for example, have a slide with bulleted text that moves in from the right side, a graphic that pinwheels in on the left side, and a title box that drops in from the top. Using the list in the Custom Animation task pane, you can set the order in which objects appear on the screen. For each object, you can choose to have it appear after you click the mouse, with the prior object, or after the prior object.

Custom animations created in older versions of PowerPoint must be converted to SmartArt for them to work in PowerPoint 2007. PowerPoint offers to convert the old animation, but the conversion isn't always perfect. Chances are you'll have to tweak the converted animation to make it work the way it did in the older presentation.

WORKING WITH CUSTOM ANIMATIONS

To animate several objects:

1. Switch to a slide you want to animate.

2. Place the objects that you want to animate on your slide.

3. Select the first object you want to animate.

4. Click Animations > Animations > Custom Animation.

   The Custom Animation task pane opens.

5. Click the Add Effect button, which displays a pop-up menu of possible effects (**Figure 10.17**). Choose an effect from the following categories:

   ▲ **Entrance** determines how the object enters the slide, including commonly used effects like Wipe and Fly In.

   ▲ **Emphasis** adds emphasis to the object. For text, that includes Change Font and Change Font Size, and for other objects, includes effects such as Grow/Shrink and Spin.

   ▲ **Exit** determines how the object leaves the slide. This includes most of the same effects as Entrance.

   ▲ **Motion Paths** creates a path the object follows. For example, you can have an object move in a line, or along a curve that you draw, or other paths. For more information, see "Animating objects along a path" later in this chapter.

   After you choose an effect from the Add Effect pop-up menu, the effect appears in the Custom Animation list.

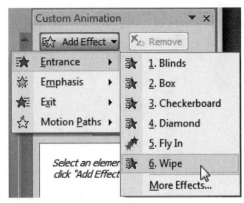

Figure 10.17 You can control how objects enter or leave the slide, whether they are emphasized, or fly them around along a path.

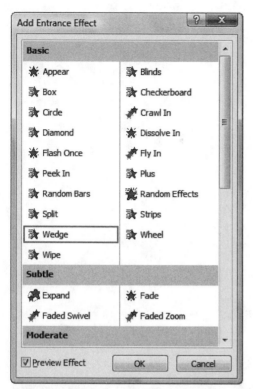

Figure 10.18 Many more objects are available from the More Effects dialog.

6. (Optional) To see more effects, choose More Effects from each category in the Add Effect pop-up menu.

An effects dialog appears, named according to the effects category you chose (**Figure 10.18**). For example, if you chose an entrance effect the dialog will be named Add Entrance Effect.

Choose an effect and click OK.

The effects dialog groups effects by style, from least obtrusive to most in-your-face (or most tasteless, depending on your point of view). The groups are Basic, Subtle, Moderate, and Exciting.

7. From the Start pop-up menu at the top of the Custom Animation task pane (Figure 10.11), choose when you want the animation to start.

8. From the Direction pop-up menu, choose the direction from which you want the object to move onto the slide.

9. Use the Speed pop-up menu to select the duration of the effect.

continues on next page

WORKING WITH CUSTOM ANIMATIONS

10. Select the next object on the slide that you want to animate, and repeat steps 5 through 9.

Every animation that you add appears in the Custom Animation list, in the order in which it will appear on the slide. When you have multiple animations, each animation in the list is numbered and the numbers also appear on your slide showing where the animations are located (**Figure 10.19**).

Animation sequence numbers don't appear during the presentation or in print.

11. To preview your animation masterpiece, click the Play button at the bottom of the Custom Animation task pane.

The animation plays in the slide area.

Animation sequence numbers

Animation sequence numbers

Figure 10.19 The animation sequence numbers appear both on the slide and in the Custom Animation list.

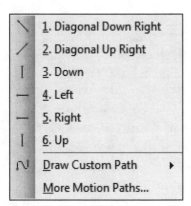

\	1. Diagonal Down Right
/	2. Diagonal Up Right
|	3. Down
—	4. Left
—	5. Right
|	6. Up
∿	Draw Custom Path ▶
	More Motion Paths...

Figure 10.20 The standard motion paths.

✔ Tips

- You can reorder the animation of objects by clicking on an object in the Custom Animation list and dragging it up or down in the list.

- To change an animation, select it in the list and click the Change button in the Custom Animation task pane. Then make your modifications as you would when creating an effect.

- To remove an animation, select it in the list and click the Remove button in the Custom Animation task pane.

- Of course, you can (and probably should) also preview your animations full-screen by playing the presentation in Slide Show mode.

Animating objects along a path

You can move objects on the slide in simple or complex paths. PowerPoint provides many preset paths, or you can draw your own. You can also customize the paths, moving the endpoints on the slide as needed.

To move an object along a path:

1. Select the object you want to animate.

2. Click Animations > Animations > Custom Animation.
   The Custom Animation task pane opens.

3. Click the Add Effect button, then choose Motion Paths from the pop-up menu of possible effects.
   Choose one of the standard paths (**Figure 10.20**).
   or

continues on next page

WORKING WITH CUSTOM ANIMATIONS

Choose Draw Custom Path, then choose Line, Curve, Freeform, or Scribble from the submenu. The cursor turns into a crosshair, allowing you to draw the path on the slide.

or

Choose More Motion Paths, which opens the Add Motion Path dialog (**Figure 10.21**). Choose a path, then click OK.

The path appears on your slide, with a green triangle showing the start of the path, and a red triangle indicating its end (**Figure 10.22**). The path doesn't appear when you print or present.

4. (Optional) You can click the endpoints of a path and drag them to adjust the path. Similarly, on some paths, clicking the path displays a selection box with handles, allowing you to change the path's dimensions.

Figure 10.21 Many additional motion paths are available from the Add Motion Path dialog.

Figure 10.22 This motion path shows the bumpy financial ride illustrated on this slide. Note the beginning (left) and end (right) points of the motion path.

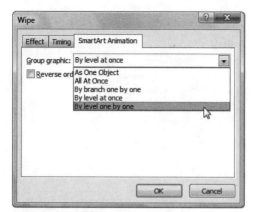

Figure 10.23 Each kind of SmartArt has its own animation adjustments.

Animating SmartArt graphics

SmartArt graphics animate in mostly the same way as other objects, but there are a few special settings to help you animate individual parts of the graphic. If you need more information about SmartArt, see Chapter 6.

To animate a SmartArt graphic:

1. Select the SmartArt graphic you want to animate.

2. Click Animations > Animations > Custom Animation.

   The Custom Animation task pane opens.

3. Use the Add Effect button and menus to add the effect as usual.

4. Click the entry for the SmartArt in the Custom Animation list, then click its down arrow and choose Effect Options from the menu.

   The Effect Options dialog appears.

5. Click the SmartArt Animation tab (**Figure 10.23**).

   This tab offers different options, depending on the kind of SmartArt graphic.

6. Make the changes you want in the dialog, then click OK.

Setting Animation Timings

Animation is movement of one or more objects over time, and so far in this chapter we've paid a lot of attention to the movement side of the equation. But the amount of time an object is moving can be crucial to make an animation look good. It should come as no surprise that PowerPoint gives you the tools to make detailed changes to the length of an animation.

Of course, PowerPoint provides some basic time settings for each animation effect with the Speed pop-up menu in the Custom Animation task pane. But you'll often want finer control. Here's how to do it.

To set an animation's time properties:

1. Select the animation effect you want to change in the Custom Animation list.

2. Click the effect's down arrow, then choose Timing from the pop-up menu.

    A dialog appears with the Timing tab selected (**Figure 10.24**). The name of this dialog will be the same as that of the selected effect.

Figure 10.24 The Timing tab gives you more fine-tuned control than the Speed pop-up menu in the Custom Animation task pane.

SETTING ANIMATION TIMINGS

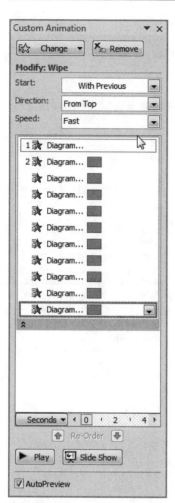

Figure 10.25 The bars next to each element of the animation indicate how long the animation is.

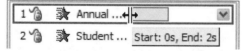

Figure 10.26 Dragging one of the orange bars lets you change the length of the animation to the second.

3. Choose one or more of the following:

▲ **Start** specifies when you want the animation to begin. Your choices are On Click, With Previous, or After Previous.

▲ **Delay** sets the length of time in seconds that should pass before the animation begins.

▲ **Speed** lets you choose from the standard PowerPoint animation speeds, from Very Slow to Very Fast.

▲ **Repeat** lets you choose the number of times you want the animation to repeat. The first option, none, makes the animation play just once. Other choices are 2, 3, 4, 5, or 10 times; until the next mouse click; or until you advance to the next slide.

4. Click OK.

To set exact animation timings:

1. Select the animation effect you want to change in the Custom Animation list.

2. Click the effect's down arrow, then choose Show Advanced Timeline from the pop-up menu.

   The Custom Animation list changes to show an orange bar next to each effect, and an overall timeline at the bottom of the list (**Figure 10.25**). The orange bar or bars in the list show the length of the animation for that element.

3. To change the length of the element's animation, point at the orange bar. The cursor changes to a double-headed arrow. Click and drag the bar to the desired length.

   A tool tip appears showing you the start and end times of the element's animation (**Figure 10.26**).

Using Action Settings

Action settings let you attach an action to a PowerPoint object. You can use an action setting to go to another slide, open a Web page, or even start another program when you click an on-screen object, or when you pass the mouse cursor over the object.

To add an action setting to an object:

1. Select the object to which you want to add an action.

2. Choose Insert > Links > Action.

   The Action Settings dialog appears (**Figure 10.27**).

3. Choose either the Mouse Click or Mouse Over tabs.

4. Choose an action from the dialog. Your choices are:

   ▲ **None**. Use this setting to remove an action setting previously applied to an object.

   ▲ **Hyperlink to** provides a pop-up menu that links to other slides in the presentation, ends the show, opens a Web page, opens another PowerPoint presentation, or opens a file on your computer.

   ▲ **Run program** opens any program on your computer.

   ▲ **Run macro** lets you choose from a list of PowerPoint macros. You must already have created a macro for this option to be active.

   ▲ **Object action** lets you open or play an embedded object, such as a media clip.

   ▲ **Play sound** lets you play a sound that you select from the pop-up menu.

   ▲ **Highlight click** highlights the selected object when you click it.

5. Click OK.

   The action setting is attached to the object.

Figure 10.27 Most of the time, you'll want to use an action setting to jump to another slide or to the end of the show.

✔ Tip

■ There is no on-screen indication that an object has an action setting attached to it. The only way you can check is by selecting the object and clicking the Action button.

Figure 10.28 PowerPoint gives you 12 pre-made action buttons.

Figure 10.29 You can't change the icon inside an action button.

Using Action Buttons

Action buttons are very similar to action settings; in fact, they also use the Action Settings dialog. The difference is that an action button is a pre-drawn shape with an icon that indicates its action. PowerPoint has 12 action buttons, covering the following actions: Back or Previous, Forward or Next, Beginning, End, Home, Information, Return, Movie, Document, Sound, Help, and Custom.

To insert an action button:

1. Display the slide where you want to put the action button.

2. Choose Insert > Illustrations > Shapes, then choose an action button from the gallery (**Figure 10.28**).

   The cursor changes into a crosshair.

3. Click and drag on the slide to create the button.

   The button appears on the slide (**Figure 10.29**).

4. Click anywhere else on the slide.

   The Action Settings dialog appears.

5. Make a choice from the dialog, then click OK to apply the action to the button you just drew.

6. (Optional) If necessary, resize and reposition the new action button on the slide.

COLLABORATING WITH POWERPOINT

You've seen in earlier chapters a bit about how you can use other applications to enhance your PowerPoint presentations. For example, in Chapter 2, you saw how Microsoft Word can be used to write the text of your presentation. In Chapter 5, there was some discussion about using graphics programs such as Adobe Photoshop and Adobe Fireworks to produce presentation images.

But importing and exporting text and pictures doesn't begin to exhaust PowerPoint's abilities to work with other applications and with your colleagues. In this chapter, you'll see how PowerPoint can use content from Microsoft Word and Microsoft Excel; and export your presentations to PDF (Adobe Acrobat) documents and other formats.

PowerPoint also has a robust commenting feature that you and your coworkers can use to add comments to a presentation while you're developing it.

Importing from Microsoft Word

Microsoft Word is the most widely used word processor in the world. Naturally, at some point you're going to want to use information that you already have in Word in your PowerPoint presentations. While there are a number of ways you can use Word documents in PowerPoint, I'm going to focus on using tables.

Of course, if all you want to do is move text from Word into PowerPoint, you can simply copy the text in Word, and paste it into PowerPoint. The text appears as bulleted text, if you paste it into a content box of a slide layout. On other layouts, the text appears as a new free text box on the slide in the default font for the presentation's theme (**Figure 11.1**).

Using Word tables

If you want to import data from tables that you have in Word documents, you can do so. The obvious reason to do this is so that you don't have to waste time retyping information from Word into PowerPoint. Another reason is to use some of the table capabilities in Word that PowerPoint lacks. For example, you can do arithmetical calculations in Word tables. You can copy the entire Word table, calculations and all, into a PowerPoint slide, or you can import just the data in the table into an existing table in PowerPoint.

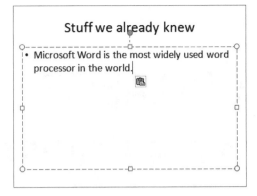

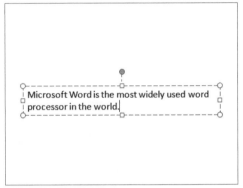

Figure 11.1 This text (top), pasted from Microsoft Word, appeared as bulleted text inside the content box of this slide layout, with the default font for the presentation's theme. On a slide with no content box, the text appears as a free text box (bottom).

Table move handle

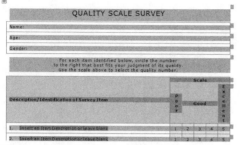

Figure 11.2 Click the table move handle in Word to easily select the entire table.

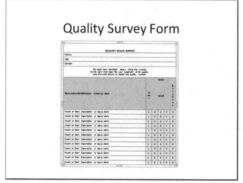

Quality Survey Form

Figure 11.3 The table appears in PowerPoint as a resizable graphic.

To import whole Word tables:

1. In the Word document, select the table that you want to move to PowerPoint (**Figure 11.2**).

   The easiest way to select the entire table is to click the table move handle, which is the square with the four-headed arrow inside it that appears when you move the mouse pointer over the table.

2. In Word 2007, choose Home > Clipboard > Copy, or press Ctrl C.

   or

   In earlier versions of Word, choose Edit > Copy, or press Ctrl C.

3. Switch to PowerPoint.

4. Display the slide where you want the copied content.

5. Choose Home > Clipboard > Paste, or press Ctrl V.

   PowerPoint's behavior is slightly different, depending on the destination:

   ▲ If you pasted onto a slide with an *empty* content box, the content box is replaced by the table.

   ▲ If you pasted onto a slide with a content box that already contains content (bulleted text, a graphic, etc.), the table appears in a layer on top of the content box.

   ▲ If you pasted onto an empty slide, or an empty area of a slide (for example, the Title Only layout), the table appears on the slide (**Figure 11.3**).

   In all cases, if you had applied any formatting to the table in the Word document, that formatting is retained in PowerPoint.

To import just the data from a Word table into a PowerPoint table:

1. In the Word document, select the data inside the table that you want to move to PowerPoint.

2. In Word 2007, choose Home > Clipboard > Copy, or press ⌃Ctrl⌃C.

   or

   In earlier versions of Word, choose Edit > Copy, or press ⌃Ctrl⌃C.

3. Switch to PowerPoint.

4. Display the slide where you want the copied content.

5. Click to place the insertion point in the first cell of the PowerPoint table.

6. Choose Home > Clipboard > Paste, or press ⌃Ctrl⌃V.

   The data from the Word table appears in the PowerPoint table.

✔ Tip

■ When the data appears in PowerPoint, it retains any formatting it had in Word. If you want to instead have it appear with the formatting of the PowerPoint table, you must reapply the table's formatting using the Design tab of Table Tools. See Chapter 8 for more information about formatting tables.

2006 National League Standings 2 [Compatibility Mode]				
	A	B	C	D	E
2006 National League Standings				
East	W	L	PCT	GB
New York	97	65	0.599	-
Philadelphia	85	77	0.525	12
Atlanta	79	83	0.488	18
Florida	78	84	0.481	19
Washington	71	91	0.438	26
Central	W	L	PCT	GB
St. Louis	83	78	0.516	-
Houston	82	80	0.506	1.5
Cincinnati	80	82	0.494	3.5
Milwaukee	75	87	0.463	8.5
Pittsburgh	67	95	0.414	16.5
Chicago	66	96	0.407	17.5
West	W	L	PCT	GB
San Diego	88	74	0.543	-
Los Angeles	88	74	0.543	-
San Francisco	76	85	0.472	11.5
Arizona	76	86	0.469	12
Colorado	76	86	0.469	12

Figure 11.4 Select the data inside the Excel worksheet.

Importing from Microsoft Excel

You'll use information from Microsoft Excel to create a table on a PowerPoint slide, or you can put Excel charts on your slides. You can bring part of an Excel worksheet into PowerPoint, or you can copy a chart in Excel and place it onto a slide.

Importing worksheet data

The best and easiest way to get worksheet data into PowerPoint is to copy the data in Excel, then paste it into a PowerPoint table. That way, you can use PowerPoint's tools to style the table the way you want, rather than deal with the formatting from Excel. Because Excel and PowerPoint have different purposes, the formatting from Excel doesn't always look great in PowerPoint, so it's best to let PowerPoint handle the formatting for the slide.

To import worksheet information:

1. On your PowerPoint slide, create a table by choosing Insert > Tables > Table, then choosing the table size you want.

   Don't worry about making the table the same number of rows and columns as the Excel data; if PowerPoint needs more room for the Excel data, it will automatically create enough rows and columns.

2. Position the table roughly where you want it on the PowerPoint slide.

   If the worksheet includes totals, you should not select them (if you do, the totals will also be charted).

3. In Excel, open the worksheet that contains your data.

4. Select the cells containing the data (**Figure 11.4**).

   If the data has row and column labels, you should select those, too.

continues on next page

IMPORTING FROM MICROSOFT EXCEL

5. In Excel 2007, choose Home > Clipboard > Copy, or press Ctrl C.

   or

   In older versions of Excel, choose Edit > Copy, or press Ctrl C.

6. Switch to PowerPoint.

7. Click the upper-left cell in the PowerPoint table to place the insertion point in it.

8. Choose Home > Clipboard > Paste (PowerPoint 2007), or choose Edit > Paste (earlier PowerPoint), or press Ctrl V.

   The Excel data flows into the PowerPoint table (**Figure 11.5**).

9. If necessary, use PowerPoint's table design tools to reformat the table to your liking. See Chapter 8 for more on formatting tables.

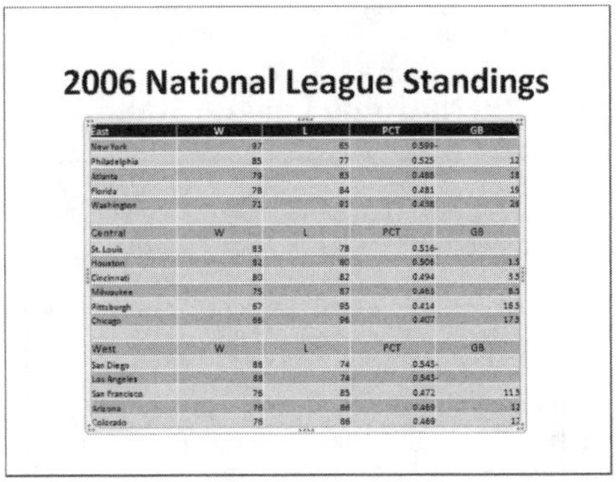

Figure 11.5 This data was reformatted inside PowerPoint, using PowerPoint's table design tools.

Figure 11.6 To move a chart from Excel to PowerPoint, first select and copy the chart in Excel.

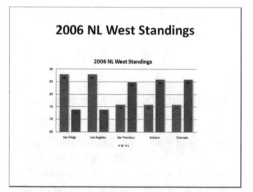

Figure 11.7 After pasting, the Excel chart appears on the PowerPoint slide.

Importing charts

As you saw in Chapter 9, PowerPoint uses Excel to create and manipulate the worksheet underlying charts that you create in PowerPoint. But you can also take charts from an Excel worksheet and paste them into PowerPoint.

To import an Excel chart:

1. In Excel, open the worksheet that contains the chart.

2. Click the chart to select it (**Figure 11.6**).

3. In Excel 2007, choose Home > Clipboard > Copy, or press Ctrl C.

   or

   In older versions of Excel, choose Edit > Copy, or press Ctrl C.

4. Switch to PowerPoint.

5. Display the slide where you want to add the chart.

6. Choose Home > Clipboard > Paste, or press Ctrl V.

   The chart appears on your slide (**Figure 11.7**).

   You'll probably have to resize and reposition the chart on the slide.

✔ Tip

■ The Excel chart will appear in PowerPoint as a chart, and if you click on it, PowerPoint's Chart Tools tab appears, with its three subtabs: Design, Layout, and Format. Using Chart Tools, you can make any formatting changes you like.

Exporting Presentations in PDF or XPS Format

If you need to export your presentation in a format that can be easily transported between computers and that can be easily printed, the correct choice is to export to PDF (Portable Document Format, also known as Adobe Acrobat format). PDF files can be viewed and printed with the free Adobe Reader, which is available for a very wide range of computer platforms, including Macintosh (Mac OS X and Classic Mac OS); Windows (3.1 through XP); Linux and other versions of UNIX; and even some handheld computers, such as Palm and Pocket PC.

PowerPoint slides that are exported to PDF generally look pretty good, but you should be aware of some limitations. For example, graphics and text in PowerPoint often turn out to look more jagged (less smooth) when exported to PDF.

An alternative to PDF is to export the file in XPS format. XPS (XML Paper Specification) is a document format developed by Microsoft as a competitor to PDF. XPS documents can be viewed using Internet Explorer 7 on Windows XP and Windows Vista. Unfortunately, as I write this (August 2007) there are no XPS viewers for the Mac or other platforms, though Microsoft promises to eventually provide them for the Mac and UNIX platforms. Unless you are certain that all of the recipients of your presentation can read and open XPS documents, I recommend that you use PDF instead.

Important: To save or export a file to PDF or XPS, you must first install the Save as PDF or XPS add-in for the 2007 Microsoft Office system. See the "Adding in PDF and XPS Support" sidebar for more information.

Adding in PDF and XPS Support

Microsoft's original intent was to build the ability to save Office 2007 documents as PDF or XPS documents into Office 2007. However, Adobe objected to this plan, because Adobe makes Windows software to convert documents running from any Windows application into PDF, and felt that Microsoft was unfairly infringing on its territory. Legal wrangling ensued, and a compromise was reached. Microsoft still offers its customers the ability to save files in PDF format, but the ability was built into an add-in that needs to be downloaded separately from Office 2007. To find the add-in, quit any Office applications that are open, then go to www.microsoft.com/downloads/. In the Search field on that page enter PDF and click the Go button. On the results page, look for "2007 Microsoft Office Add-in: Microsoft Save as PDF or XPS." Download and install the add-in file, then re-open PowerPoint. PDF or XPS will now be an option under Office Button > Save As.

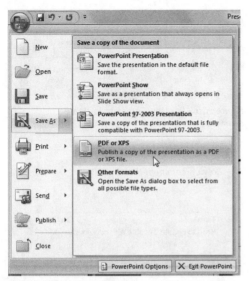

Figure 11.8 After downloading the appropriate add-in, it's easy to save your presentation as a PDF file.

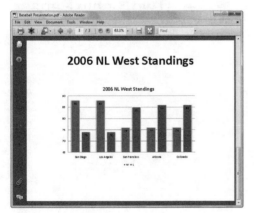

Figure 11.9 Here's the exported PDF file in Adobe Reader.

To export a presentation to PDF or XPS:

1. Open the PowerPoint file that you wish to export to a PDF or XPS file.

2. Choose Office Button > Save As > PDF or XPS (**Figure 11.8**).

   The Publish As PDF or XPS dialog appears, prompting you for the name of the exported PDF or XPS file and where you want to put it on your hard disk.

3. Give the document a name, and if necessary, navigate to the directory where you want the document to go.

4. From the Save as type pop-up menu, choose either PDF or XPS document.

5. Click Publish.

   The Publishing window appears, and shows you the progress of the export.

   When the publishing is complete, the document opens in the designated viewer for the file type you selected, for your review (**Figure 11.9**).

✔ Tip

■ Presentation files exported to PDF can be quite large, especially if you have many photographic images in the slideshow. Large files are often not convenient to send via email, or to post on the Web for downloading. If all you need are lower-resolution images for use online or via email, click the Minimum size (publishing online) button in the Publish As PDF or XPS dialog. This applies extra compression to the images, reducing the overall file size.

EXPORTING IN PDF OR XPS FORMAT

Working with Comments

If you're working as part of a team to create a presentation, you might want to insert notes to other team members. In PowerPoint, comments work like electronic sticky notes that you can place anywhere on your slides. You can use them to remind yourself of missing or questionable info or keep track of where you left off work. Comment boxes are always labeled with the name and initials of the person who added the comment. This is a built-in workaround for the fact that PowerPoint, unlike Word and Excel, doesn't have a function to track changes. But you can add, edit, delete, and step through comments in your presentation.

To add a comment:

1. In the Normal View Pane, scroll to and select the slide on which you want to place the comment.

2. To add a comment about text or an object on a slide, select the text or object. If instead you want to add a general comment about a slide, click anywhere on the slide.

3. Choose Review > Comments > New Comment (**Figure 11.10**).

   A new comment box appears on the slide, with your name (PowerPoint asked for your name during product registration) and the date.

4. Enter your text in the comment box (**Figure 11.11**). To save the comment, just click anywhere else on the slide.

   When you click outside the comment box, the comment box collapses to the review comment thumbnail.

✔ Tip

■ Comments don't appear on screen when you give the presentation.

Figure 11.10 Click New Comment to create a new comment.

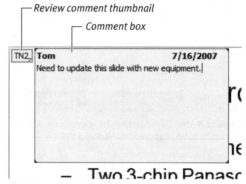

Figure 11.11 Type your comment into the comment box.

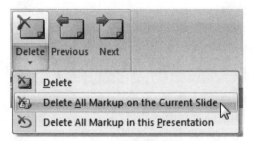

Figure 11.12 To delete multiple comments, make a choice from the Delete pop-up menu.

To view comments:

◆ Hover the mouse pointer over a review comment thumbnail. The comment appears while the mouse pointer is over the thumbnail, like a tool tip.

or

Click a review comment thumbnail.

The comment box appears, and it doesn't disappear until you click somewhere else on the slide or on a different slide.

or

Choose Review > Comments > Next.

This brings you to the next comment, whether it is on the current slide or not. Repeat this command to step through all the comments in the presentation.

To edit comments:

◆ Double-click a review comment thumbnail.

or

Click to select a review comment thumbnail, then choose Review > Comments > Edit Comment.

The comment box opens, with the insertion point at the end of the existing text.

To delete a comment:

1. Click a review comment thumbnail to select it.

2. Choose Review > Comments > Delete.
The comment disappears from the slide.

To delete multiple comments:

1. Under Review > Comments > Delete, click on the arrow to bring up the pop-up menu (**Figure 11.12**).

2. Choose "Delete All Markup on the Current Slide" or choose "Delete All Markup in this Presentation."
If you choose the latter, PowerPoint will display a dialog asking if you're sure you want to delete all comments. Click Yes.

Emailing your Presentation

PowerPoint makes it easy to share your presentation with colleagues via email.

To email your presentation:

1. Save your current presentation.

2. Choose Office Button > Send > E-mail (**Figure 11.13**).

   Your default email program will launch and create a new email message, with your presentation file attached (**Figure 11.14**).

3. Address and send the email as you ordinarily would.

✔ Tip

- The Send submenu also allows you to email the presentation as a PDF attachment or an XPS attachment. This saves you the extra step of having to first save the presentation in one of those formats before you email it.

Figure 11.13 The Office Button's Send menu allows you to email your presentation in a variety of formats.

Figure 11.14 When you send the presentation as an attachment, PowerPoint creates a new message in your default mail program (in this case it is Windows Mail).

EMAILING YOUR PRESENTATION

Exporting Presentations as a Web Page

You can make your presentation available to the widest audience by converting it into a Web page and placing it on a Web server, either on the Internet or on your company's intranet. The presentation will be readable in one form or another by anyone with a Web browser on any major computing platform (Windows, Mac, Linux, and others). Unfortunately, Microsoft adds proprietary code to the Web page that makes the presentation look best in Internet Explorer. If you need to have the presentation appear exactly as it does on screen, consider saving it as a PDF file, as discussed previously in this chapter.

Presentations turned into Web pages resemble Normal View, with the outline on the left, a large area for the slide, and a space for Speaker Notes (**Figure 11.15**).

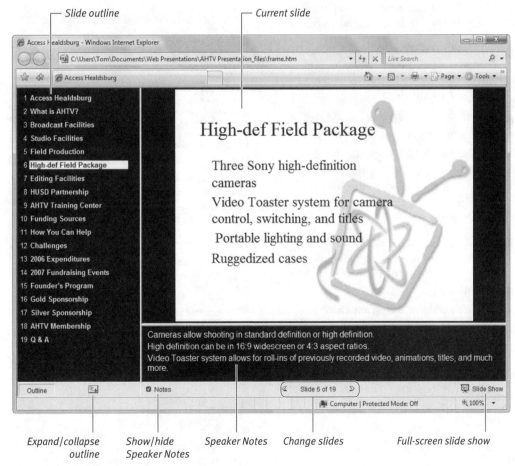

Slide outline   Current slide

Expand/collapse outline   Show/hide Speaker Notes   Speaker Notes   Change slides   Full-screen slide show

Figure 11.15 If you view it in Internet Explorer, a PowerPoint presentation exported as a Web page looks pretty good.

To convert your presentation into a Web page:

1. Save the presentation.

2. Choose Office Button > Save As > Other Formats.

3. In the Save As dialog, choose Web Page from the Save as type pop-up menu (**Figure 11.16**).

   PowerPoint automatically fills in the file name and the Web page's title with the name of the presentation.

4. To accept all of PowerPoint's defaults for publishing your presentation, click Save. Most of the time, however, you'll want to make changes, so follow the steps below.

5. (Optional) You can edit the file name by changing it in the Save As dialog, and you can edit the page title by clicking the Change Title button.

6. (Optional) To adjust PowerPoint's default settings for Web pages, click Publish.

   The Publish as Web Page dialog appears (**Figure 11.17**). In this dialog, you can choose whether or not to display your Speaker Notes on the Web, publish only certain slides, and more.

7. (Optional) For even more control over your new Web page, click the Web Options button in the Publish as Web Page dialog.

   The Web Options dialog appears (**Figure 11.18**). It's a good idea to make the files on a Web site smaller, and you can do that by telling PowerPoint to make the Web page for a modern version of Internet Explorer.

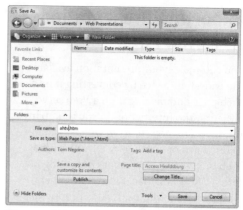

Figure 11.16 You need to select Web Page from the Save as type pop-up menu.

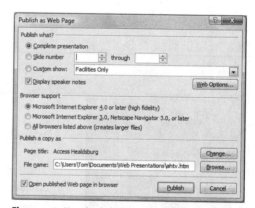

Figure 11.17 Use the Publish as Web Page dialog to export all or part of your presentation, and to include (or not) Speaker Notes.

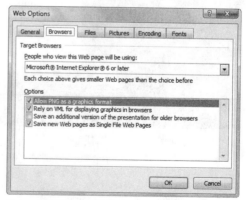

Figure 11.18 The Web Options dialog allows you to fine-tune your export settings.

8. (Optional) In the Web Options dialog, click the Browsers tab, then choose Microsoft Internet Explorer 6 or later from the "People who view this Web page will be using" pop-up menu.

9. When you're done setting the options, click OK to leave the Web Options dialog, which returns you to the Publish as Web Page dialog. Click Publish.

   PowerPoint converts the presentation to a Web page. The saved Web page will consist of two parts. One is the HTML file, and the other is a companion folder with the files that make up the presentation (text, graphics, etc.).

10. You need to copy the Web page and the companion folder to a Web server for it to be viewable by others. If you don't know how to do that, ask your Web site's administrator.

✔ Tip

■ If you choose to put your Speaker Notes on your Web site, make sure that you review them first. Since Speaker Notes aren't normally seen by the audience, you might have notes that make sense to you but not to your audience. Or you might even have notes that you would rather not share with your audience. To keep your Speaker Notes from appearing on the Web, uncheck "Display speaker notes" in step 6 above.

Exporting Presentations as Image Files

If you need to use your slides in another program—such as a page layout program—you can export your slides as image files, with one image per slide. You can choose the format of the image files. In ascending order of quality, you can export slides as GIF, JPEG, PNG, or TIFF files.

To export a presentation as image files:

1. Open the PowerPoint file that you wish to export to image files.

2. Choose Office Button > Save As > Other Formats.

3. In the Save As dialog, choose one of the image formats from the Save as type pop-up menu.

4. Click Save.

   PowerPoint asks if you want to export every slide in the presentation or only the current slide (**Figure 11.19**).

5. Click Every Slide or Current Slide Only.

   PowerPoint creates a new folder with the presentation's name and puts the exported slides into it (**Figure 11.20**).

Figure 11.19 When you export the presentation as image files, PowerPoint asks what the scope of the export should be.

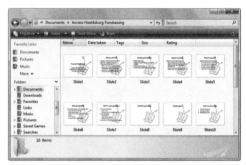

Figure 11.20 PowerPoint exports each slide in the presentation as individual image files.

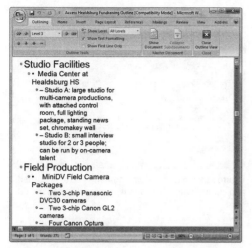

Figure 11.21 If you like, you can open the exported PowerPoint outline in Microsoft Word for further editing.

Exporting the Presentation Outline

Sometimes you want to extract just the text of your presentation, so you can use it in a Word document, or for use in another program, such as a page layout program. You might also want to send just the outline in an email. PowerPoint allows you to export the presentation's outline (as seen in Outline View) in Rich Text Format (RTF), which is an interchange format that retains text formatting, and can be read by many different programs on virtually all computing platforms.

To export the presentation outline:

1. Open the PowerPoint file that you wish to export as an outline.

2. Choose Office Button > Save As > Other Formats.

3. In the Save As dialog, choose Outline/RTF from the Save as type pop-up menu, navigate to where you want to save the outline file, and if needed, give the file a name other than the default one PowerPoint provides.

   Click Save.

   PowerPoint saves the outline text. If you open the text in Word's Outline View, you'll see that slide titles and bulleted text are presented in outline form (**Figure 11.21**).

✔ Tip

■ Speaker Notes are not retained with the outline when you export it as an RTF file.

Saving the Presentation to CD

PowerPoint 2007 allows you to turn your presentation into a package, which is a folder or a CD that contains all of the files associated with your presentation, including graphics, the PowerPoint file, fonts, external movies linked to the presentation, and sounds. The package also contains a copy of the PowerPoint Viewer program, so the recipients of the CD don't even have to have PowerPoint installed to admire your work.

The reason why you want to create a package, rather than just copy the presentation file to a CD, is that you need to make sure that all of the elements of your presentation come along with the file. To be efficient and to make sure the PowerPoint presentation file doesn't get too big, PowerPoint invisibly links large external files (especially video files) into the presentation, but does not copy those files into the presentation file. Similarly, fonts that you have on your system may not be available on another computer, and creating a PowerPoint package copies the fonts used in the presentation for use by the PowerPoint Viewer.

To package your presentation for burning to a CD:

1. Open the presentation you wish to burn to CD.

2. Choose Office Button > Publish > Package for CD.

   The Package for CD dialog appears (**Figure 11.22**).

3. In the dialog, if you don't like the default name of PresentationCD, you can change it.

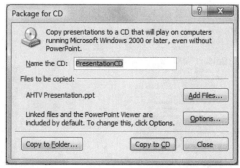

Figure 11.22 In this dialog, name the CD to be burned, and choose which files you want to include on the CD.

Figure 11.23 The Options dialog lets you fine-tune your CD package's contents.

4. (Optional) You're not limited to copying only one presentation file to the package; if you want to add additional presentations, click the Add Files button, then use the resulting Add Files dialog to choose the presentation files.

5. (Optional) By default, the PowerPoint Viewer and linked external files will be included in the package, and all the presentations in the package will play automatically when the CD is inserted. To change this, click Options.

   The Options dialog appears (**Figure 11.23**).

6. (Optional) Select one or more of the following choices:

   ▲ To change how the presentations play in the Viewer, select one of the choices in the pop-up menu under Viewer Package.

   Your choices are Play all presentations automatically in the specified order; Play only the first presentation automatically; Let the user select which presentation to view; or Don't play the CD automatically.

   ▲ If you don't want to include the PowerPoint Viewer, choose Archive Package, rather than the default Viewer Package choice.

   ▲ If you don't want to include linked files or embed fonts in the package, clear those checkboxes.

   ▲ If you like, you can enter passwords that will be required to either open or modify the presentation files included with the package.

   When you're done setting options click OK. You will return to the Package for CD dialog.

   continues on next page

7. To burn the package to a CD, click Copy to CD.

If there isn't a CD already in the drive, PowerPoint will ask you insert a blank CD. Do so, then click the Retry button.

After the CD is burned, PowerPoint asks if you want to make additional CDs. Make your selection.

or

To save the package as a folder on your hard drive (which you can copy to a network server, or even burn to a CD later), in the Package for CD dialog click Copy to Folder. In the resulting dialog, give the folder a name and browse to the location on your hard drive where you want to save it, then click OK.

✔ Tips

■ If PowerPoint tells you that it isn't able to burn the CD, it may be because your computer has CD burning software that is incompatible with direct burning from PowerPoint. That doesn't mean you can't burn a CD with your presentation. The workaround is to save the package as a folder on your hard disk, then use your CD-burning program to copy the folder to a CD.

■ Before you save the presentation to a CD, make sure that the presentation's settings are as you want them, especially if you've created Custom Shows. The show selected in Slide Show > Set Up Show will be the one that plays in the PowerPoint Viewer.

■ Always preview the contents of the CD before you send it off!

■ The PowerPoint Viewer program works only on Windows. If you want to share your presentation with a Mac user, save the package as an Archive Package on your hard disk, then copy the resulting folder to a hard drive, USB thumb drive, or burn it to a CD. Your friend will have to have either PowerPoint for Mac or Keynote installed to view the presentation, of course.

GIVING THE PRESENTATION

The funny thing about presentations is that you do a bunch of work to create your presentation and make it look good, and at the end of the process the real job hasn't even started yet—you still have to give the presentation. For some people, giving a presentation (and public speaking in general) ranks in popularity just this side of dental surgery. Other folks like nothing better than to be standing in front of an audience. Most of us, however, fall somewhere between the two extremes.

Luckily, people have been speaking in front of groups for thousands of years, and there is a lot of received wisdom about what you can do to make giving a presentation a comfortable experience for both you and your audience. Besides the nuts and bolts of giving a presentation with PowerPoint, I'll include some speaking tips in this chapter that should help improve your presentations.

You'll also learn how to give presentations with laptops and external monitors or projectors; use PowerPoint's Presenter View; discover some cool hardware and software extras for presentations; and print your presentation so that your audience can bask in the glory of your presentation long after you've disappeared into the night.

Preparing to Present

The more presentations you give, the better a speaker you will be. The key to giving a good presentation is to be prepared, pay attention to the details, and have plenty of practice. Here are some tips that can help your overall presentation.

Before the presentation

◆ Before you give a presentation, get a friend or coworker to read through it. You'll be surprised at how often they'll find a typo or awkward grammar that you missed.

◆ Try hard not to run over your allotted time. It's always a good idea to practice your presentation using a clock, stopwatch, or PowerPoint's Presenter View to see how long your presentation is. It's much better to cut slides before the presentation than to run out of time and not be able to finish at all. On the other hand, if your presentation is running short, it's better to find out before you're in front of a bunch of expectant faces.

◆ Speaking of practice, make sure that you build enough time into your preparation schedule so you can practice the presentation, out loud, at least twice before you give it. By the way, practicing your presentation means giving the entire presentation just as you would in front of an audience. It doesn't mean quickly riffling through your PowerPoint file half an hour before you hit the stage.

I recommend that you give the presentation in front of one or two trusted associates twice. The first time, your friends can stop you during the presentation and make suggestions or ask questions. Then you should incorporate their feedback and, if necessary, tighten up the presentation. The second time, give the presentation exactly the way you plan to give it to your audience. Your associates can take notes and give you feedback at the end. But you absolutely need the experience of giving the entire presentation all the way through before you give it for real.

♦ Things do go wrong; your notebook computer could die before you give your show, or could have video problems with the venue's projectors. Make sure that you keep a backup copy of your presentation file on something other than your notebook. I prepare two backup copies of important presentations; one on a USB drive, and another on either an iPod or burned to a CD. That way, if I get to the venue and my notebook goes south, I can borrow a computer and still go on with the show.

♦ When you make your backup copies, if your presentation contains any video files, don't forget to also copy those video files into the same folder as your presentation. PowerPoint doesn't embed video files into the presentation file; instead it links to the external video files. See Chapter 7 for more information about using video in your presentations.

PREPARING TO PRESENT

Giving the presentation

◆ If you can, get to the presentation venue a little early. Sit or stand where you will be when you're speaking, and make sure that your seating (or the podium) is adjusted the way that you want it. Take a moment to adjust the microphone and work with the venue's audio technician to get the levels right before the audience arrives. Make sure you have a spot to place a cup of water. Getting comfortable with the physical space and the facilities helps a lot.

◆ If you have the opportunity to greet some of the audience members as they enter the room, you should do so. It's easier to speak to people you know, even if all you've done is say hello.

◆ If you're speaking at a conference and you are wearing a conference badge or pass around your neck, take it off before you begin your talk. It will often reflect stage lights back at the audience, which can be distracting.

◆ Before you begin, visualize yourself giving a successful presentation. Imagine that you've spoken very well, and see in your mind the audience's involvement in your talk. Hear their applause, and picture audience members coming up to congratulate you after the show. It sounds a bit silly, but visualizing success works.

◆ Concentrate on your message, not on the audience. If you focus on what you're saying, you will distract yourself from being nervous.

◆ If you are nervous, never apologize for it. Except in extreme cases, most audiences don't notice that speakers are nervous, and it doesn't help your case to point it out.

◆ Always keep in mind that your audience *wants* you to succeed. People don't go to a presentation thinking, "I sure hope this guy gives a lousy talk and wastes my time." They want to get something out of your presentation as much as you do.

◆ Unless you are a professional comedian, keep the jokes to a minimum, or skip them altogether. A joke that falls flat isn't a good way to start a show.

◆ Never read straight from a script. Very few people can read from a script without putting their audience to sleep; we call those people actors (and professional speakers).

◆ Don't read your slides aloud word for word. Your slides should be signposts and reminders of what you want to say. Using your slides as your teleprompter is another way to lose audience interest. For prompts, use your Speaker Notes.

◆ It's a good idea to put a summary slide at the end of your presentation. Not only does it bring your talk to a natural end, but it helps to once again drive your argument home to your audience.

◆ After the presentation is over, thank your audience and make yourself available for questions. As you are chatting with people, get feedback from them so that you can improve the next show. Simply asking them if there was anything they would have liked you to cover can yield useful information.

PREPARING TO PRESENT

Cool Presentation Gear

As already noted in this book, what matters is what you're saying in your presentation. But there is a variety of hardware and software that can make giving the presentation easier, more convenient, or both.

Cool hardware

The first bit of hardware that should be on your list is a **laser pointer**. These handy items are perfect for drawing the audience's attention to a part of your slide, and they're essential if you will be doing a demonstration on the computer as well as the slideshow. They are widely available for as little as $10. I think that the $100 lasers with a green beam are especially cool, but that's because I'm a presentation geek.

One of the drawbacks to doing presentations with a computer is that you are usually tied to the location of the computer. For some presenters, especially people who are more comfortable if they can move around as they speak, a **remote control** is the answer. These units consist of a handheld control and some kind of receiver that usually connects to your computer via the USB port. Some remote controls use infrared as the connection between the handheld unit and the receiver, and others use RF (Radio Frequency). Infrared remotes require a line of sight between you and the receiver, and the remote can control your computer from a distance of between 20 and 30 feet. RF controllers can work even if you can't see the computer (they can even work through walls), and have a slightly greater range, up to 40 feet. Don't forget to bring extra batteries for your remote control to the presentation!

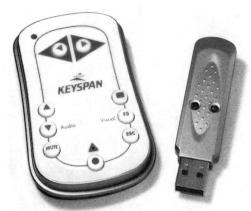

Figure 12.1 The Keyspan Easy Presenter lets you control PowerPoint and the volume of your computer's playback.

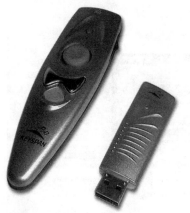

Figure 12.2 Keyspan's Presentation Remote has a touchpad that allows mouse movement and includes a laser pointer.

There are many remote controls available, starting at about $40 and zooming up to as much as $120. The two remote controls I've used the most are both made by Keyspan (www.keyspan.com). The $40 RF Easy Presenter (**Figure 12.1**) controls PowerPoint, and includes a built-in laser pointer and audio controls. The Keyspan Presentation Remote (**Figure 12.2**), an RF device that sells for $60, has a joystick-like touchpad that provides full mouse control, and includes a laser pointer.

You might already have a remote control for your Mac in your pocket, without even knowing it. If you have a Windows Mobile, Palm, Sony Ericsson, Motorola, or Nokia **cellular phone** with Bluetooth capability, you can use it as a remote control for PowerPoint and many other programs on your PC with the help of a terrific software package called Salling Clicker (see "Cool software," below). Bluetooth connections are good for about 30 feet from your PC, and they do not require line of sight.

If you need to transport your presentation between computers, you can burn it onto a CD, or you can use a **USB flash drive**. These units are about as long as your thumb, and plug into any USB port. They provide up to 4 GB of storage, with no moving parts, and are powered by your computer. When you plug the flash drive into your computer, it shows up on the desktop, just as any other drive does. I put my presentation files on mine as a backup, so I know that even if my notebook dies, the show can go on with a borrowed computer. If you have an iPod shuffle, which is a USB flash drive, you can reserve some of its capacity for your files (later model iPod shuffles require you to use a docking cable for file storage, so don't forget to pack that).

Cool software

There are a few software packages that can enhance the presentation process or work around some of PowerPoint's limitations:

◆ **Salling Clicker**, from Salling Software (www.salling.com), is a great program that allows you to use your Windows Mobile, Palm, Sony Ericsson, Motorola, or Nokia mobile phone or PDA with Bluetooth to remotely control a wide range of applications, including PowerPoint (**Figure 12.3**). The program uses scripts to control programs, so the more script-able an application is, the more that Salling Clicker can do with it. The included scripts for PowerPoint let you play a presentation, go to the first, last, previous, or next slide; or toggle the screen to black.

The nice thing about using your cell phone as a remote control, of course, is that you don't have to carry around a separate remote control.

◆ **iPresent It** lets you skip using PowerPoint altogether to give your presentation—if you have an iPod with photo and video output abilities and you don't mind a presentation that is only a series of still images without animations. iPresent It converts your PowerPoint presentation into JPEG files and then syncs them to your iPod (**Figure 12.4**). You hook your iPod up to a television or a projector, and you can step through your slides. You can find iPresent It at www.zapptek.com.

Figure 12.3 Salling Clicker lets you use your Bluetooth-enabled mobile phone as a remote control.

Figure 12.4 You can play your presentations from an iPod with iPresent It.

Skipping Slides on Playback

There are times when you have your presentation ready to go, and you arrive at the venue and realize that you don't want to show some of the slides in your presentation. Perhaps your company's product line has changed, and you want to hide the slide that shows the fabulous Wonder Widget because it will soon be replaced by a new model (probably the Ultra Wonder Widget). Sometimes even news reports are a reason to remove slides from your presentation; for example, you probably wouldn't have wanted to give a presentation with a picture of a sinking ship the day after the *Titanic* went down.

You must select slides to be hidden before you begin the presentation; you can't choose to hide a slide while you are playing the presentation.

To set slides to be hidden:

1. Open your presentation.

2. If PowerPoint isn't already in Normal View, click the Normal View button at the bottom of the PowerPoint window, then click the Slides tab in the Normal View Pane.

3. In the Slides tab, click to select the slide that you want to skip.

   You can select multiple slides by clicking the first slide that you wish to skip, holding down the Shift key, and clicking the last slide in the selection. You can select discontiguous slides by selecting the first slide, holding down the Control key, and then selecting subsequent slides.

continues on next page

SKIPPING SLIDES ON PLAYBACK

4. Right-click one of the selected slides, then from the resulting shortcut menu, choose Hide Slide.

PowerPoint marks the hidden slides by dimming them in the Slides tab and putting a box with a slash through it over the slide number (**Figure 12.5**).

✔ Tips

■ You can also hide a slide by selecting it and clicking Slide Show > Hide Slide.

■ To restore a skipped slide to your presentation, select the slide thumbnail in the Slides tab, right-click, and choose Hide Slide again from the shortcut menu.

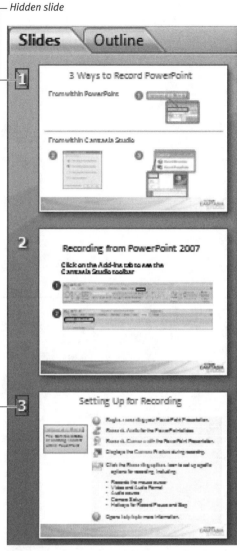

— Hidden slide

Hidden slide ——

Figure 12.5 After selecting a slide in the Slides tab and setting it to be hidden, PowerPoint dims the slide content and puts a box with a slash through it over the slide number.

Setting Up the Projector

Most presentations are viewed by being projected onto a large screen, but you can also show them on your computer screen, or on a second monitor connected to your computer. When you're using a second display (either a second monitor or a projector) you are using *multiple monitors*, where the presentation plays on the second display, and your display shows you PowerPoint's Presenter View (more about that later).

When you're using a notebook computer to give your presentation, your computer must support multiple monitors. To use multiple monitors on Windows, you must be running Windows Vista, Windows XP, or Windows 2000 SP3 or later. Your notebook must also have a VGA video output (most do). You'll view the presentation on your notebook screen, and your audience will view the projected screen.

Hook the projector (if you don't have a projector, you can use another external display, such as a monitor) up to the notebook. Most PC notebooks have a VGA port, but some require an adapter; check the documentation for your notebook.

Exterior displays, whether a monitor or projector, should be VGA compatible, and capable of displaying at either 800 x 600 or 1024 x 768 resolution.

SETTING UP THE PROJECTOR

To set up multiple monitors:

1. Connect the second display to your computer.

2. To configure your computer for multiple monitors in Windows Vista, right-click the desktop, then choose Personalize from the shortcut menu. The Personalize control panel appears. Click Display Settings, and the Display Settings dialog opens (**Figure 12.6**).

   or

   If you're using Windows XP, right-click the desktop, and choose Properties. The Display Properties dialog appears. Click the Settings tab.

   The two monitors will appear as icons in the dialog. The notebook screen is by default the primary monitor (labeled with a 1).

3. Click the icon for the second monitor, click "Extend the desktop onto this monitor" (on Windows XP, click "Extend my Windows desktop onto this monitor,") and then click Apply.

   The second monitor should now show your desktop wallpaper.

4. Using the Resolution slider (**Figure 12.7**), choose the screen resolution that matches the resolution of the projector display. It will typically be either 800 X 600 or 1024 X 768. Click OK to save your settings.

Figure 12.6 When you have two displays connected, there are two monitor icons in Display Settings.

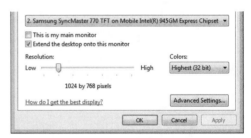

Figure 12.7 Set the resolution of the external projector or display.

SETTING UP THE PROJECTOR

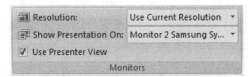

Figure 12.8 If you want to have different things appear on your notebook screen and the presentation screen, you'll need to enable Use Presenter View in PowerPoint.

5. Now that you are set up for multiple monitors, you need to tell PowerPoint that you'll be using a projector. Open your presentation in PowerPoint, then choose Slide Show > Monitors > Show Presentation On, then choose the projector from the pop-up menu (**Figure 12.8**).

6. If you want to use the Presenter View during your presentation, click the Use Presenter View checkbox. To learn more about Presenter View, see "Using the Presenter View," later in this chapter.

✔ Tips

- It's usually a good idea not to run PowerPoint while you're setting up multiple displays. Sometimes the change in video modes confuses PowerPoint, and you have to quit and relaunch it to make things work again.

- If your laptop doesn't sync with the projector (the image doesn't appear on the projector or is distorted), shut down, then restart the computer with the projector connected. This usually fixes the problem.

SETTING UP THE PROJECTOR

Running the Presentation

Now that the presentation and the projector are ready to go, and the audience has arrived, it's time to get your presentation going. During the presentation, you can control your show with the keyboard.

To run your presentation:

1. In the Normal View Pane, click to select the first slide in the presentation.

2. Click the Slide Show button at the bottom of the PowerPoint window (**Figure 12.9**).

   or

   Choose Slide Show > Start Slide Show > From Beginning, or Slide Show > Start Slide Show > From Current Slide (**Figure 12.10**).

   or

   Press F5.

   The slideshow begins. Click the mouse button, or use the right arrow key to advance through your slides.

3. At the end of the show, by default PowerPoint will go to a black screen; click the mouse button to leave Slide Show mode and go back to the PowerPoint window.

   or

   To end the slideshow manually, press Esc.

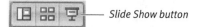

Slide Show button

Figure 12.9 To run the presentation, click the Slide Show button at the bottom of the PowerPoint window.

Figure 12.10 Choose from which point you want to begin your presentation.

Table 12.1

Keyboard Controls during Presentations	
ACTION	KEY(S)
Play the presentation	F5
End the presentation	Esc
	- (hyphen)
Next slide or animation	Mouse click
	Enter
	Right arrow
	Down arrow
	Page Down
	N
	Spacebar
Previous slide or animation	Left arrow
	Up arrow
	Backspace
	Page up
	P
First slide	Home
	1+Enter
Last slide	End
Toggle black screen	B
	. (Period)
Toggle white screen	W
	, (Comma)
Go to the first or next hyperlink on a slide	Tab
Go to the last or previous hyperlink on a slide	Shift-Tab
"Click" the hyperlink	Enter (while a hyperlink is selected)

Keyboard controls during the show

When you're running the slideshow, PowerPoint gives you some control over the show's progress by letting you press keys on the keyboard and click the mouse. See **Table 12.1** for a list of controls.

✔ Tips

- Table 12.1 isn't a complete list of keyboard controls during the show; I've omitted rarely used controls. To get a complete list, while running your presentation, press the F1 key. You'll get the Slide Show Help window, which lists all of the possibilities (**Figure 12.11**).

- I usually use the spacebar to advance slides or slide animations when I present, because it's the biggest and easiest to find by touch while I'm talking.

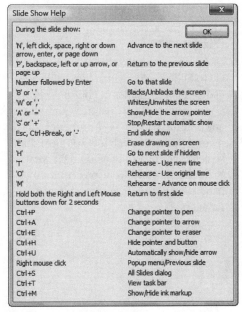

Figure 12.11 The Slide Show Help window shows your options during the presentation.

Controlling and Annotating the Presentation

During the presentation, if you're not using the Presenter View, PowerPoint provides some onscreen tools that you can use to control your show. They include ways to move to the previous and next slides, a menu that allows you to jump to any slide or custom show in your presentation, a way to pause your presentation or turn the screen black for a moment, and a tool that allows you to draw on the presentation screen (**Figure 12.12**).

These controls appear at the bottom-left corner of the screen when you move the pointer over them. They are unobtrusive icons, so as not to attract too much audience attention.

To control the presentation:

◆ To advance to the next or previous slides, click the Next slide or Previous slide icons.

or

Click the Control menu icon.

The Control shortcut menu appears (**Figure 12.13**).

Of particular note in this menu is the Go to Slide choice, which has a submenu listing all of the slides in your presentation, allowing you to instantly jump to any point in your show. Another useful menu is Screen, which lets you turn the screen Black or White; you might want to do that to pause your presentation to handle a question from the audience, for example.

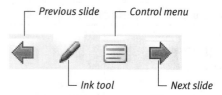

Figure 12.12 When you're not using Presenter View, control icons appear in the lower-left corner of the screen.

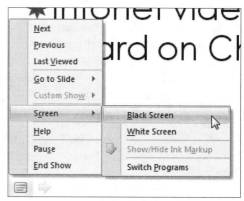

Figure 12.13 The Control menu allows you to skip to other slides or blank the screen for a brief pause.

Figure 12.14 Choose from various weights and colors for your annotations in the Ink tool menu.

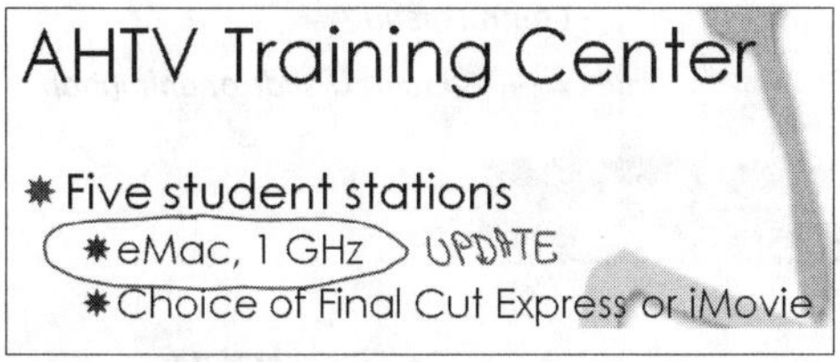

AHTV Training Center

* Five student stations
* eMac, 1 GHz   UPDATE
* Choice of Final Cut Express or iMovie

Figure 12.15 The annotation tools let you circle and scrawl brief notes on your screen.

To annotate the presentation:

1. Click the Ink tool icon.

   The annotation menu appears (**Figure 12.14**).

2. Choose the kind of drawing tool you want; your choices are Ballpoint Pen, Felt Tip Pen, or Highlighter.

3. (Optional) Choose the ink color you want from the Ink Color submenu.

4. Click the slide and draw or write your annotations (**Figure 12.15**).

5. At the end of your show, when you end the presentation, PowerPoint presents a dialog asking if you want to save your ink annotations. Click either the Keep or Discard buttons.

✔ Tips

■ You'll usually use the notebook's track-pad or a mouse to do the annotations, but if you're presenting from a Tablet PC, you can use the stylus.

■ If you keep slide annotations, they become part of your presentation, as a graphic overlaid on your slide. If you want, you can erase these annotations in Normal View simply by selecting them on the slide and pressing Backspace.

Using the Presenter View

The Presenter View allows you to view your presentation and display your Speaker Notes using an interface that only you see. It gives you a control panel that you see on your notebook's screen, while the audience sees the regular slideshow on the projector. This mode is only available when you are using multiple monitors.

In Presenter View, you get a scrolling list of your slide thumbnails, a large view of the current slide, buttons for Previous Slide and Next Slide, your Speaker Notes, and best of all, an onscreen timer that tells you the elapsed time of your presentation (**Figure 12.16**). This timer is a great tool to help you stay on track; by knowing how long you have been talking, you can speed up or slow down to keep within your allotted speaking time.

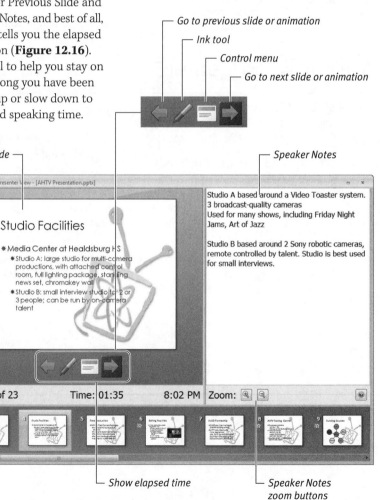

Go to previous slide or animation

Ink tool

Control menu

Go to next slide or animation

Current slide

Speaker Notes

Slide thumbnails

Show elapsed time

Speaker Notes zoom buttons

Figure 12.16 The Presenter View gives you a view of your presentation that the audience doesn't see.

To activate Presenter View:

1. Set up your computer for multiple monitors. See "Setting Up the Projector," earlier in this chapter, if you need help.

2. Choose Slide Show > Monitors > Use Presenter View checkbox.

3. In Slide Show > Monitors, choose the projector from the Show Presentation On pop-up menu.

To use Presenter View during the presentation:

◆ Click the Next or Previous buttons to go forward or back in the slide deck.

◆ Click any slide thumbnail to jump directly to that slide. If there is a slide transition associated with the slide you clicked, it will trigger and the slide will appear on the projector.

◆ Adjust the size of the Speaker Notes display by clicking one of the two Speaker Notes zoom buttons.

◆ Click the Ink tool to annotate your slide.

◆ Click the Control menu to apply any of its functions. See "Controlling and Annotating the Presentation" earlier in this chapter for more information.

USING THE PRESENTER VIEW

Creating Custom Shows

Have you ever needed to show part of a presentation, but not all of it, for a particular audience? For example, let's say that you have a presentation about a new product that includes slides with commission rates for the sales department. When you give the presentation to the marketing department, you can omit the commission slides by creating a *custom show*. This is a subset of the presentation that includes just the slides you want.

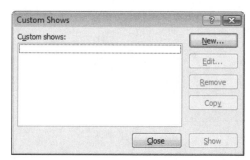

Figure 12.17 Begin creating a custom show in this dialog.

To create and use a custom show:

1. Open your presentation.

2. Choose Slide Show > Custom Slide Show > Custom Shows.

   The Custom Shows dialog appears (**Figure 12.17**).

3. Click the New button.

   The Define Custom Show dialog appears (**Figure 12.18**).

4. Name the custom show, then select slides from the list on the left, and click the Add button in the middle of the dialog to add them to the list on the right.

5. Click OK, and then, back in the Custom Shows dialog, click Close.

6. To run the custom show, choose Slide Show > Custom Slide Show. In the resulting pop-up menu, choose the show you want.

   The custom show runs.

Figure 12.18 Custom shows must be named, and you can add just the slides you want.

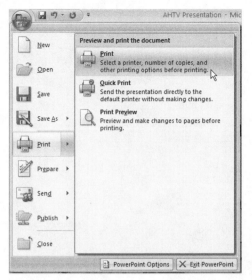

Figure 12.19 Choose Print from the Office Button to bring up the Print dialog.

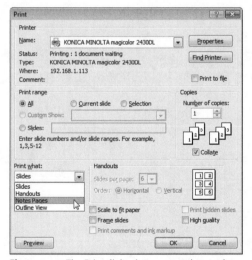

Figure 12.20 The Print dialog lets you set the number of copies and the page range for the print job.

Printing Your Presentation

Most of the time, your presentation will come to life on a monitor or when projected for your audience. But it's quite common to be asked to provide your presentation in printed form as well. Printed presentations are often used as audience handouts. PowerPoint allows you to print your slideshow in several different ways to meet a variety of needs. You can print just your slides; your slides with your Speaker Notes; a handout, which is a layout that prints between two and nine slides per page; or you can print the slideshow's outline.

Printing slides is a good way to proof your presentation. Presentations look different on paper than on-screen, so proofing print-outs allows you to catch errors that you otherwise might have missed.

To print your slides:

1. Open the presentation you want to print.

2. Choose Office Button > Print > Print (**Figure 12.19**).

    The Print dialog appears (**Figure 12.20**).

    continues on next page

3. In the Print what section, choose one of the following:

▲ **Slides** prints just the slides, one per page. Slides will print in landscape orientation, to maximize their size on the paper.

▲ **Handouts** prints 1, 2, 3, 4, 6, or 9 slides per page. If you choose Handouts, the Handouts section of the dialog becomes active, and you can pick the number of slides per page and whether they will be ordered horizontally or vertically. The 3-slide layout includes lines next to the slides for audience notes.

▲ **Notes Pages** prints one slide per page, with your Speaker Notes below the slide.

▲ **Outline View** prints the presentation's outline, without slides.

4. From the Color/grayscale pop-up menu (not visible in Figure 12.20 because it is hidden by the Print what pop-up menu), choose the color option you want:

▲ **Color** prints the slide as it appears on screen on your color printer.

▲ **Grayscale** discards the color, but retains backgrounds, gradients and other visual effects, such as shadows.

▲ **Pure Black and White** turns the slide backgrounds to white, turns all text to black, and hides text and object effects. However, photographs, clip art, and the charts are still printed in grayscale.

By default, PowerPoint sets the printer to Color or Grayscale depending on your printer's capabilities.

5. Select the print formatting options that you want:

   ▲ **Scale to fit paper** shrinks or expands the slides to fit your paper size.

   ▲ **Frame slides** puts a thin border around the edges of each slide.

   ▲ **Print hidden slides** prints all slides in the Slides tab, whether or not they are marked as hidden.

   ▲ **Print comments and ink markup** prints any ink annotations on the slides.

   ▲ **High quality** prints shadows on text in Color or Grayscale print modes. Choose this option if you want your slide printouts to look exactly like your slides; on the other hand, a drop shadow that looks good on a screen may not look great from your printer. Do a test print and make a choice.

6. (Optional) If you want to see a preview of your slides before they go to the printer, click the Preview button.

   PowerPoint switches to its Print Preview mode. Click Print Preview > Preview > Close Print Preview to leave this mode.

7. (Optional) If you want to print just a portion of the presentation, make choices in the Print range section of the dialog.

   PowerPoint will present you with a Save dialog so you can choose where to save the PDF file.

8. Click OK to print.

✔ Tips

- It's almost always a good idea to preview the slides on screen (see step 6) before you print them.

- If you output the presentation as a PDF file, you can use the full version of Adobe Acrobat to add annotations, hyperlinks, and other enhancements.

- Unfortunately, you cannot customize PowerPoint's print layouts. So if you want a layout with six slides to a page, and with lines for audience notes, you're out of luck, at least printing from PowerPoint. One alternate possibility would be to create a custom layout by taking screenshots of each slide, then creating the layout in a page layout program such as Adobe InDesign or QuarkXPress.

INDEX

3-D rotation effect, 103, 104

A

Acrobat, Adobe, 209, 216, 252
action buttons, 207
action settings, 206
Action Settings dialog, 206
activating program, 2, 3
activation form, 2, 3
ActiveX controls, 134
Add Effect button, 198, 201, 203
Add-Ins tab (Ribbon), 8
Add Motion Path dialog, 202
Add Shape menu, 117
Add Sound dialog, 191
Adjust group, 101, 102
Adobe
    Acrobat, 209, 216, 252
    Flash movies, 134
    InDesign, 252
    Photoshop, 101
    Photoshop Elements, 101
    Reader, 216, 217
AIFF files, 124, 127
Align menu, 89
Align Text buttons, 67
Align Text Vertically command, 67
aligning
    graphics, 34–35
    objects, 89
    table cell contents, 155
    text, 34–35, 56, 66–67, 155
Alignment group, 155
All Programs menu, 2, 3
alpha channels, 81
animated logos, 134
animation effects, 192–205
    applying, 192–193
    avoiding overuse of, 190
    controlling, 194, 195, 204–205
    customizing, 193–195, 196. *See also* custom
        animations
    defined, 185
    moving objects along paths, 201–202
    previewing, 200, 201
    removing, 201
    reordering, 201
    repeating, 205
    setting direction for, 194, 199
    setting speed/timing for, 194, 199, 204–205
    for several objects, 198–201
    for SmartArt graphics, 203
animation formats, 134
animation presets, 192, 193, 196
animation timings, 204–205
Animations tab (Ribbon), 8, 188
annotation tools, 245
Apple
    GarageBand, 129
    QuickTime, 133
    QuickTime Pro, 133
Archive Package option, 228
area charts, 162
Arrows fly-out menu, 100
attachments, email, 220
AU files, 124
Audacity, 129
audience handouts, 31
audio editing programs, 129
audio file formats, 124, 127
audio recording software, 128, 129
AVI files, 133
axes, chart, 163, 164
Axes group, 175, 178
axis labels, chart, 175

B

Back button, 207
background images, 157
background music, 123
Background Styles gallery, 47
backgrounds
    slide layout, 46–48
    table cell, 157–159
backup copies, 231
Ballpoint Pen tool, 245
Banded Columns option, 148
Banded Rows option, 148
bar charts, 162, 164, 174, 175
Beginning button, 207
bevels, 104, 157
Blank layout, 39, 46, 140, 165

E

F

G

O

objects
  aligning, 89
  animating, 197–203
  attaching actions to, 206
  distributing, 89, 90
  flipping, 88
  grouping/ungrouping, 91
  layering, 93
  modifying outlines for, 99–100
  placing images within, 98
  positioning, 85, 92
  resizing, 84–85
  rotating, 87–88
Office 2007
  activating programs, 2, 3
  built-in templates, 39
  clip art, 80
  diagramming feature, 109
  font rendering in, 58
  Graph program, 166
  new features, 5
  presentation program, 1
  Reduced Functionality mode, 3
  registering programs, 2, 3
  Research pane, 30
  Save as PDF or XPS add-in, 216
  text handling in, 49
  themes, 37
  trying out, 2
  WordArt, 106
Office Button, 4, 6
Office Theme, 16, 20
OpenType fonts, 59
outdents, 75
Outline/RTF option, 225
Outline tab (Normal View Pane), 5, 23
Outline View, 23, 24–26
outlines (presentation), 24–29
  benefits of using, 24, 27
  exporting
    as RTF files, 225
    to Word from PowerPoint, 225
    from Word to PowerPoint, 29
  moving headings in, 26
  printing, 250
  purpose of, 24
  styling text in, 25
  writing
    in Microsoft Word, 28
    in Outline View, 24–26
outlines (shape/picture), 99–100
Outlining shortcut menu, 26
Outlook, 5, 37, 109, 121

P

Package for CD dialog, 226, 228
packages
  creating, 226–228

  defined, 226
  fine-tuning contents of, 227
  and Macintosh, 228
  naming, 226
  saving, 228
page layout programs, 252
Palm cellular phones, 235, 236
Paragraph dialog, 71
Paragraph group, 58, 66–67
paragraph spacing, 71
paths, animating objects along, 201–202
PC notebook computers, 239. *See also* notebook
    computers
PC remote controls, 234–235
PDF files
  exporting presentations as, 216–217, 221
  meaning of acronym, 216
  printing, 216, 252
  sending as email attachments, 220
  viewing, 216
  vs. XPS files, 216
Pen Color pop-up menu, 152
Pen Style pop-up menu, 152
Pen Weight pop-up menu, 152
phones, Bluetooth cellular, 235
photo editing programs, 101
Photo-Objects 150,000 package, 82
Photoshop, 101
Photoshop Elements, 101
PICT files, 81
picture adjustment tools, 101
Picture Border command, 99
Picture Bullet dialog, 74
picture bullets, 74
Picture button, 80
picture captions, 55
Picture Effects menu, 104
picture fills, 158
Picture Styles gallery, 103
Picture Tools tab (Ribbon), 84, 101, 102, 103
Picture with Caption layout, 39
pictures. *See also* graphics; images
  applying effects to, 104
  applying styles to, 103
  cropping, 86
  exporting SmartArt as, 121
  inserting, 80–81
  modifying, 101–102
  outlining, 99–100
pie charts, 162, 164, 174, 179–182
Pie Explosion slider, 180
Plantronics, 128
Play Across Slides option, 126, 133
Play Full Screen option, 133
Play Movie pop-up menu, 133
Play Sound dialog, 127
Play Sound pop-up menu, 125
plot area, chart, 163, 164, 166
PNG files, 81, 121, 224
podcasts, 129

Publish As PDF or XPS dialog, 217
Publish as Web Page dialog, 222

Q

QuarkXPress, 252
Quick Access Toolbar
    customizing, 11–12
    location in main window, 4
    purpose of, 6
QuickTime, 133
QuickTime Pro, 133

R

radar charts, 162, 164
Radio Frequency Infrared remotes, 234
Radio Quality setting, 130
Reader, Adobe, 216, 217
Recolor tool, 101
Record Narration dialog, 129
Reduced Functionality mode, 3
reference materials, 30
reflection effect, 103, 104, 157
Reflection gallery, 104
registering program, 2, 3
registration key, 2, 3
remote controls, 234–235
Rename button, 44
Rename Layout command, 47
Replace window, 77
Research pane, 30
Reset command, 41
Reset Graphic command, 116
Reset Picture tool, 101
Reset to Match Style command, 174
Resolution slider, 240
Return button, 207
Review tab (Ribbon), 8
Rewind Movie After Playing option, 134
RF controllers, 234
RF Infrared remotes, 234
Ribbon
    how it works, 8–9
    introduction of, 5
    location in main window, 4
    minimizing, 10
    purpose of, 5
    tabs on, 8. See also specific tabs
rich media, 123. See also specific types
Rich Text Format, 225
Rotate handle, 55
rotation handles, 87
rows (chart)
    deleting, 169
    hiding/unhiding, 169
    moving, 168
    relabeling, 167
    transposing data in, 171
rows (table)
    defined, 140

deleting, 146
evening out spacing of, 145
inserting in tables, 147, 149
resizing, 144
selecting, 143
setting number of, 141
royalty-free clip art, 82
RTF files, 225
rulers, 34, 75, 76, 92

S

Salling Clicker, 235, 236
Save as PDF or XPS add-in, 216
Save As Picture dialog, 121
Save As Template command, 184
Save Chart Template dialog, 184
scaling graphics, 84
scatter charts, 162
Science Fair Project template, 19
Screen menu, 244
screen resolution, 239, 240
Section Header layout, 39
Select pop-up menu, 143
selection handles, 84, 142, 149
Send Backwards command, 57, 93
Send menu, 220
Send to Back command, 57, 93
sentence case, 63
shading, 157
shadow font style, 61
shadows, 157. See also drop shadows
Shape Effects gallery, 105
Shape Fill gallery, 95
Shape Outline command, 99
Shape Outline gallery, 99
Shape Styles gallery, 94
Shape Styles group, 174
shapes
    adding images to, 98
    adding text to, 97
    adding to SmartArt, 117–118
    applying effects to, 105
    defined, 80
    deleting, 83
    filling, 94–96, 98
    outlining, 99–100
    placing, 83
Shapes gallery, 83
Size and Position dialog, 85, 87, 88
Size dialog, 84
Size group, 85
skipping slides, 237–238
Slide Layout gallery, 39, 40
slide layouts, 37–48
    adding placeholders to, 44
    applying, 20, 40–41
    changing background for, 46–48
    for charts, 165
    customizing, 18, 38
    defined, 15

INDEX